In Fandom's Shadow

Being a Doctor Who Fan from the 1990s to Today

Aaron John Gulyas

Deserted Moon Press

Grand Blanc, Michigan

2013

First published 2013 by Deserted Moon Press

DEDICATION

For James and Andy

CONTENTS

1 What are We Doing Here? 1

2 History of My Fandom 6

3 Fiftieth Anniversary Binge: An Introduction 19

4 The 1960s 21

5 The 1970s 31

6 The 1980s 42

7 The 1990s 54

8 The New Series 61

9 Out from the Shadow 70

10 Past and Future in *Doctor Who* 76

Recommended Reading 93

ABOUT THE AUTHOR

Aaron Gulyas is a historian, writer, and associate professor of history at Mott Community College in Flint, Michigan, where he teaches all manner of courses, as well as serving as a part-time educational technology consultant for the college's Professional Development office.

Gulyas's newest publication is *In Fandom's Shadow: Being a Doctor Who Fan from the 1990s to Today*-- a brief ebook exploring aspects of Doctor Who in light of its 50th anniversary. His first book, *Extraterrestrials and the American Zeitgeist: Alien Contact Tales Since the 1950s* was published by McFarland Books in May, 2013. He contributed the introduction to *Posthuman Blues: Dispatches From a World on the Cusp of Terminal Dissolution*, a collection of writings by the late Mac Tonnies edited by Paul Kimball and published by Redstar Books. Recently, he had a chapter appear in Gillian I. Leitch's Doctor Who in Time and Space.

He is currently writing *The Chaos Conundrum: Essays on UFOs, Ghosts, and other High Strangeness in our Nonrational and Atemporal World* for Kimball Books as well as a great deal of history and educational freelance writing.

1
WHAT ARE WE DOING HERE?

What the world needs now, more than anything, is another independently published unauthorized book about *Doctor Who.*

It is the fiftieth anniversary, after all, so why not more more *Doctor Who* themed items? After all, we have DVDs, posters, t-shirts, and sonic screwdrivers to fit every budget. There are more episode guides than I ever would have thought possible, in an age when all of the most basic information is contained somewhere on the Internet (and, at the risk of sounding like a sycophant, none of them are better than Tat Wood and Lawrence Miles's *About Time* series).

So what's this for, and who do I expect to be reading this?

Partially, it's an effort to set down--as much for myself as anyone else--a record of my *Doctor Who* fandom. That's, admittedly, an odd and somewhat egocentric goal, but I have a strange fear. I feel like I'm a member of something of a lost generation. I came to *Doctor Who* after its initial run's end in 1989. I never viewed the series in order or in any kind of thorough obsessiveness until quite recently. As the title suggests, I grew up in the shadow of a fandom which had in many ways taken control of the *Doctor Who* master narrative. Fanzine articles, as well as the *Archive* features and *Off the Shelf* review columns in *Doctor Who Magazine* laid down tracks upon which my views of the show--at least initially--would run. In an era before I had access to the Internet or to any dedicated guidebooks, a different sort of fandom—that of general American "cult TV" fandom and its narrow, limited view of *Doctor Who*—also shaped my knowledge of the show's history.

This is a journey of discovery. It is a story of a teenage boy finding himself in love with a television show and a mythology at a time when it was, perhaps, far more difficult than it is now. It's also the tale of the power of popular culture to transcend national boundaries and at the same time accentuate boundaries of time and space. I became a fan on the wrong continent in the wrong decade. The story is divided into several parts.

First, is something for which I have failed to come up with a clever name ("autowhobiography" was the closest I came--I gave up after that). It's the autobiography of my *Doctor Who* fandom; how I discovered the show and, having discovered it, delved into its lore, and persuaded others (well, one or two) to join him on this horrific quest to the heart of a show that was, and is, far far more than it seems. Like the TARDIS, it's truly bigger on the inside. Then, I move deeper into the story and discuss the so-called Wilderness Years, that period in the 1990s and early 21st century when there was no new televisual *Who*, apart from the FOX/Paul McGann...um...thing, *The Curse of Fatal Death*, and (sob) *Dimensions in Time*. What we did have, early on anyway, were the *New Adventures* series of novels, published by Virgin. This was my era of the show, the one I come back to again and again and which fills me with considerably more feelings of nostalgia than much *Who* from earlier or later.

The new series arrived in 2005, however, and was beyond my wildest expectations. I wondered, however, if it could ever be as good as the old stuff. "Good", of course, being a relative term. To put the new series in perspective, this year (2013), in honor of the show's 50th anniversary, I embarked on an epic, ill-advised, expensive ("well, sure I need the Special Edition DVD of 'The Visitation'...") and time-consuming re-watch of every extant episode, in order. It was, as you'll hopefully see, something of a revelation. What I thought I liked, what I certainly *remember* liking, I found dull and irritating. Serials (and whole eras) I was dreading reviewing ended up being much more enjoyable than I ever imagined.

So that, generally, is the "what." The "why" is less straightforward. I'm an historian by training and trade and I worry that some things--including first-hand accounts of these sorts of personal interactions with the ephemera of popular culture--might be lost to future generations. I'm also a pessimist. *Doctor Who*, 2005-present, will not last forever. Fans of the show, who grew up with Christopher Eccleston, David Tennant, Matt Smith, and [insert doc12 here!] will fall away in great numbers. Those who persist in their fandom will face their own wilderness years. My *Who* story--like those of countless others of my generation--may, perhaps, be part of a roadmap of hope for those wandering souls.

A bit pretentious. I'll try again. This is also a "you kids get off my lawn" exercise. I was talking to a young person a while ago, who enjoys the new *Doctor Who* (and is getting into the older stuff as well). She was shocked and a bit frightened to learn that at one time here in the

United States, there was no practical way to obtain *Doctor Who* merchandise without great time and expense. She can walk into nearly any store that caters to geek consumers (itself a recently discovered and exploited market segment) and buy all manner of *Doctor Who* material. She said to me, "It took a lot of dedication to be a fan back then." This got me thinking about the value of being a fan of something--an author, television show, band, sports team, whatever. Our interests and our--yes--obsessions help define our personality and our relationships with those around us and in the age of the Internet, help define our relationships with others around the world. I decided that this was worth exploring from a perspective that was more personal than a scholarly investigation.

So, in general, there we have it. This isn't an episode guide or a blow-by-blow catalogue of my reactions to every episode of *Doctor Who*. This is an anecdotal meander through growing up a geek at a time when that was even more difficult than it is now. It is a tale of scraping together pocket change to buy *Doctor Who* books I read about in newsletters and magazines only to discover that my local bookstore could not get its hands on them for any amount of money. It's about the elation and serendipity of finding old Target novelizations in the strangest places. It's about *Doctor Who* being broadcast on my local PBS station in the middle of the night, and the way I invariably fell asleep in the middle of every Jon Pertwee story. It's about trying to write fan fiction (before I even heard the term or imagined that anyone else would want to do that) and finding through the process that fiction is something that was best left to other people. It's about the feeling that no matter how good the new BBC Wales series is, it's jut *not* the same.

2
HISTORY OF MY FANDOM

There is a prelude to my *Doctor Who* fandom that occurred on a Sunday afternoon around 1985 or so (as far as I can remember). I was about ten years old, flipping through the five available channels in our antenna-equipped home and I found something very strange which had wolf men, green slime, and lots of volcanoes. I watched, fascinated but unable to understand anything that was going on. Eventually, I gave up because it had been on for hours and it was time for supper. I know now that I was watching "Inferno," probably my favorite Jon Pertwee story but it didn't grab me at the time.

That would happen a bit later, in January 1991. Looking through the newspaper's television listings one Saturday evening, I saw the following:

Doctor Who **(WFWA 39, 10:00 PM): "Ghostlight" The Doctor and Ace arrive in a Victorian mansion where aliens in the cellar plot to assassinate Queen Victoria.**

Well, who *wouldn't* want to watch a show with that description? In the Saturday 10:00 PM slot, I had been watching *Twin Peaks*, which I barely understood but which seemed very cool. This "Doctor Who" show sounded much, much cooler. I tuned in and for 75 minutes I was absolutely enthralled with the dialogue and look of the story. I couldn't really follow the plot, but the characters of the Doctor and Ace seemed well-developed. There was humor, there was an ending which made sense given what I had been watching, and I felt a compulsion to watch the show again the next week. That story (as you, dear reader, probably know) was *The Curse of Fenric*, and following that was *Survival.* I loved every one of these stories and was thrilled to have found a show that, to my knowledge, **no one else in the universe** seemed to have heard of. I looked forward to seeing what the next story would bring.

I duly tuned in at 10:00 PM the next Saturday and was...confused. The show was called *Doctor Who*, but it was...old. In color, but with a tall white haired guy that no one on the show even recognized as the Doctor. The story was called "Spearhead from Space" and it was really enjoyable, but I had no idea what was going on. Where was the little Scottish sounding guy? Where was Ace (who I missed more than the little Scottish guy, to be honest)? I had a mystery to solve.

Unlike people today, I had to go to a library. With books and stuff. Being a good library type of fellow, I looked through the card catalog for books about science fiction television shows. I found a few which discussed *Dcotor Who*, amongst other shows that were science fiction, British, or British science fiction. The information I found, however, was sparse. I found that *Doctor Who* began in 1963 and featured a lead character which could change his form when his body became damaged beyond repair. He travelled with a variety of companions and his most popular form was a tall curly haired, scarf-wearing guy named Tom Baker.

It wasn't much, but it was enough to start investigating further. With no internet at my disposal, I was years away from finding a publication which listed every *Doctor Who* story in order from 1963 to...when? I had reasoned out that "Survival" was the most recent episode (none of the books I had been able to find even mentioned this "Sylvester McCoy" guys and most seem to have been published around 1986, possibly the high water mark of US interest in *Doctor Who*) but was there more beyond that 1989 episode? I had no way to know.

What I did find, much to my delight, was that the Allen County Public Library system held in its collections dozens of novelizations of *Doctor Who* stories published by WH Allen and Target books. I began to piece together a picture of the series as a whole from reading these and, to a degree, began to formulate a list of likes and dislikes in my mind. I liked the first Doctor--although I was confused by the Doctor having *three* companions--but the library had few of the sixth Doctor stories (specifically, "The Twin Dilemma," "The Two Doctors," and "Timelash") so I was unable to get a handle on that era. Soon, I began to find *Doctor Who* novelizations at local book stores and, although distribution to US stores was terrible, was able to order them as well. In particular, the Spy-Sci Fi catalog, issued by Larry Charet of Chicago, was a source for many, many purchases of books and magazines when I was in high school. In the days before widespread video releases and when my local PBS station seemed to insist on showing the same stories I'd seen over and over and over, the Target novelizations were the primary way I experienced the show.

Doctor Who Magazine was the other. This was harder to come by but far more informative than the novelizations. For some reason, *Doctor Who* fandom has always seemed more interested in the production side of the show's history than have fans of programs such as *Star Trek*. Andrew Pixley's "Archive" features in the 1990s *DWMs* were eye opening and, often, if I had some money designated for *Doctor Who* merchandise I was far more inclined to seek out back issues of the magazine than novelizations. The video reviews in the magazine also affected my perceptions of stories I had not yet seen, coloring my opinions when I finally did. It was because of the articles in DWM that I was predisposed to have a negative opinion of some stories. The final Tom Baker story, "Logopolis," for example, was a story I was less than excited to see, based on my readings of Gary Russell's review of the BBC video release, which referred to "Logopolis" as "four episodes of pretentious, frequently unintelligible, overrated, glossy waffle" which "could have been told far more economically in about two episodes." [1]). At the same time, elsewhere in that issue, there was an article which made "Logopolis" (and the rest of season 18) sound like the best bunch of *Doctor Who* stories ever. I was intrigued and ever more eager to seek out that story.

The factual articles about the behind the scenes production details of stories did as much to whet my appetite for getting my hands on actual video as did the

1. Doctor Who Magazine #185

novelizations or reviews of stories. In particular, the path a story took from initial idea to final script (and how that script changed when confronted with the physical, financial realities of making *Doctor Who* in the 1960s, 70s, and 80s) made me want to see these stories more than anything else, to determine if I could detect the changes the plot, characters, or setting had gone through.

Within a year or so of becoming a *Doctor Who* fan I had discovered a fairly local fan group, the Whoosier Network (a pun, of course, on "hoosier," the traditional nickname for people living in Indiana). I was too far from any of the places where the group had local meetings but I enjoyed the newsletter well enough. Some of the people who wrote for it, though, seemed a little excitable, taking issue with those who had *any* negative opinions of *any* aspect of the show. Even though I was new to the whole thing, I certainly thought that all *Doctor Who* was not created equal. I was not, for example, a fan of the vast majority of Jon Pertwee stories (too long, too boring, too much the same from week to week) and there was so much I hadn't seen that I did not feel equipped to offer an opinion. I knew, at a certain level, that reading the Target novelization was not the same as seeing the shows. The view that all *Doctor Who* was equally good because it was all *Doctor Who* was as wrong-headed as thinking all *Star Trek* was good, despite the existence of episodes like "Spock's Brain" or "Spectre of the Gun."

At this early stage of my fandom I didn't know what the *Doctor Who* equivalent to those horrible stories might be, but I suspected there must be. If I was to believe books like Peter Haining's *25 Glorious Years* (which my friend Andy and I jointly owned on an odd sort of "time share" basis) and *Doctor Who: A Celebration*, then the historical stories (except "Marco Polo" and "The Aztecs") were largely lousy and unpopular, which is why they stopped making them after "The Highlanders." The limited range (in the US) of stuff to buy also annoyed me. I didn't want posters or props. I wanted books and magazines. I wanted to find the obscure novelizations that I couldn't get locally, or the newest issues of *Doctor Who Magazine*. Other American fans--at least those I encountered--did not seem to have as much interest in these things as I did.

One interesting aspect of fandom that I only briefly (and horribly) dabbled into was writing fan fiction. Today, there are countless websites, blogs, and the like dedicated to fans crafting their own unauthorized, unofficial tales of the Time Lord and his friends. Before I even knew it was an actual activity people engaged in, I thought it would be fun to write a *Doctor Who* story. I don't think I actually finished one. I am—

no false modesty here—*terrible* at making things up. Fiction is something best left to those with some sort of talent.

I have no real recollection of everything I tried to write. I recall a story with the Doctor (seventh?) and Nixon, wherein Nixon had beaten John F. Kennedy in the election 1960. This result had (with characteristically fannish hyperbole) led to nuclear war. Unless I'm misremembering, I plotted the Sontarans in as the cause of this historical anomaly (I still think it's a better use of Nixon in *Doctor Who* than "The Impossible Astronaut"/"Day of the Moon").

I also remember Andy and I coming up with a six-story outline of how we'd bring back *Doctor Who* if it were up to us (two American high school students so, you now, it was *possible*). After looking all through my files, I don't have the document we produced but I seem to remember a historical episode set during the Bolshevik Revolution as well as a battle between the Daleks and the Cybermen. I am fairly certain that we planned to regenerate the Doctor, just because we could.

I have found, in recent years, that my perceptions about the difference between American fans (as I was exposed to them in the Whoosier Network newsletter and elsewhere) and British fans (as I was exposed to them in

Doctor Who Magazine, other fanzines I got my hands on, and so on) were not just my view. Tat Wood, in the 6th volume of the excellent and massive *About Time* series of books about the history of the series addressed this issue as well. In the essay, "Did They Think We'd Buy Just any Old Crap?" Wood asserts that some of the *Doctor Who* gear being produced in the United States

> *was embarrassingly gushing. Some of it was slickly-produced, and could have been for any show, just with Peter Davison's face stuck on it. All Doctor Who was judged as good (except the black and white stories they hadn't yet shown in America, in which case the fane took the unjustified party line and said that. . ."The Gunfighters" was terrible and. . ."The Celestial Toymaker" was perfect)."* [2]

Thus I tended to gravitate toward not hanging out with other *Doctor Who* fans unless I was actually friends with them before I started watching the show. I had no interest in watching the show with groups of people with whom I had nothing in common other than the fact that we were all in a room watching *Doctor Who.* For me, *Doctor Who* was a mostly solitary activity.

---

2. Tat Wood. *About Time: The Unauthorized Guide to Doctor Who.* Volume 6. Des Moines, Iowa: Mad Norwegian Press, 2007, 75.

One important exception to this non-fraternization-with-other-fans trend was when Andy and I attended Whoosiercon II in Indianapolis on March 28, 1992. The entire trip was a birthday present from my parents who, to their credit, did not do much to discourage my increasingly time- and money-consuming *Doctor Who* habit. My dad drove me and my friend Andy to a hotel on the west side of Indianapolis (about two hours away) and left us there for the whole day to meet Sylvester McCoy, Sophie Aldred, Craig Charles (Lister from *Red Dwarf*) as well as some other alleged celebrities. For us, though, the highlight of the whole thing was probably the merchandise room, where I purchased many, many back issues of *Doctor Who Magazine* and Andy bought far more Target novelizations than is medically advisable. If I recall correctly, he actually bought enough from one vendor to negotiate some sort of bulk discount.

While I was able, week-by-week, to view stories that were new to me and, through libraries, borrowing from Andy, and judicious use of pocket money able to absorb as many novelizations as humanly possible, it was not enough. I still felt like I was missing out on the entire *Doctor Who* experience, as I was unable to take part in the show a first-run phenomenon. More and more, as I forming my opinions I realized I was unable to form an opinion in the way other older (and, crucially, British, fans had. For me, coming to it in 1991, *Doctor Who* was a complete package. In its televised form, it had a beginning, middle, and end. I would never be able to experience the show as a continuing narrative. With the show on an indefinite hiatus, it seemed unlikely that I would *ever* be able to.

Virgin Publishing, in 1991, came to my rescue with a new series of original novels called the New Adventures. They featured the seventh Doctor and Ace, with whom I had started the journey, and would be--we were told--deeper, more complex, and more "adult" than the novelizations had been. The tagline from the publisher--"stories too broad and deep for the small screen"--seemed to be just what I was looking for. The first few novels were parts of a linked series wherein the Doctor and Ace battled the Timewyrm. They were okay--certainly *Doctor Who*-ish (especially Terrence Dicks's *Timewyrm: Exodus*). The fourth and final book in the opening series, however, was mind-bending.

Paul Cornell's *Timewyrm: Revelation* was the first New Adventure that simply would not have been possible to be made as a television show. Taking place in a variety of locations including Britain, the Moon, and insid the Doctor's psyche (!), it explore the Doctor literally from the inside out. Previous incarnations of the Doctor made cameo appearances, but not in the literal-minded style of anniversary stories like "The Five Doctors." Rather, in Cornell's book, the past selves of the Doctor formed an allegory, each representing an aspect of the overall character. *Timewyrm: Revelation* was the first time I got the impression that *Doctor Who* was (or, at least, in the right hands *could* be) more than a cheap-looking-but-fun television show. Cornell's book showed me a depth of thinking that I never got from the Target novelizations and certainly did not perceive in spin-off novels based on other franchises, particularly the dire and simplistic *Star Trek* novels of the early 1990s. The series of books would run through the mid-1990s, being an integral part of my high school and college leisure reading. While I was in college, another crucial building block in my development as a fan was the advent of an increasing number of factual books. These ranged from the informative and serious (like the "Handbook" series of episode guides by Howe, Stammers, and Walker, who also produced the excellent fanzine *The Frame*) to fictional (Lance Parkin's *History of the Universe*, now expanded upon as *AHistory*) to humorous (Chris Howarth and Steve Lyons's *The Completely Useless Encyclopedia*).

Thus, between the old stories, the New Adventures, and the behind the scenes information and commentary provided by *Doctor Who Magazine* and various factual works, I was becoming far more knowledgeable about

Doctor Who than I was about nearly anything else. Looking back, this was not ideal. During certain semesters of college I am sure that I spent more time reading *Doctor Who* books than I did reading the materials required for my classes. The sheer volume of new *Doctor Who*, in text form at least, that appeared during the 1990s made me feel like I was part of an ongoing series for the first time.

In 1996, though, the arrival of the Fox TV Movie starring Paul McGann as the short-lived eighth Doctor was an event which very nearly blew my tiny mind. The internet (still a recent development) served up endless speculation, spoilers, and publicity photographs to the point where I thought I simply *could not wait* for the May 1996 premier of the movie. As it happened, I was studying abroad in Italy on the day it was broadcast, necessitating a very expensive phone call to my parents to remind them to tape the TV movie. I remember emphasizing that they should *under no circumstances* attempt to pause the recording during commercials, lest they forget to *un*-pause and cause me to miss valuable *Doctor Who.*

I will be discussing the TV Movie more later in the book but when it was not continued into a series, as we had all hoped, I have to admit that my enthusiasm diminished a bit. At the same time, Virgin's line of New

Adventures ended within a year of the television movie. [3]Instead, the BBC launched their own line of original novels featuring the eighth Doctor. These were, for whatever reason, more difficult to find in the US than the Virgin books had been and, in any case, were not as good (in my opinion, at least). *Doctor Who* began to take a backseat to other interests. I drifted back toward *Star Trek*, finishing my undergrad degree, and finding a job. *Doctor Who* was there, but in the background, with not a lot of my money being spent on it between 1998 and 2003 or so.

In 2003, of course, came the announcement that the series would be returning for thirteen episodes in the Spring of 2005, with a lavish budget all under the guiding hand of Russell T. Davies, *Doctor Who* fan, New Adventures author, and (most importantly) well-regarded television writer and producer. Suddenly, I was excited again. Regardless of what the new series looked like or whether it continued past the initial thirteen episodes, it was the greatest shot *Doctor Who* had to return in the way it always should have--weekly, on Saturday, on the BBC. Watching the show here in the States was an issue at first, until it was picked up by US cable networks. Now, with BBC America and

---

3. At least for the Doctor. His companion Bernice would continue to star in the series for several years afterward.

iTunes, getting the show is no problem. In 2005, though, I was worried that there would be be new *Doctor Who* and I would not be able to see it. Surely, this would be a fate worse than death.

In the end, we Americans were able to see it and, suddenly, there was new *Doctor Who* again. For the first time since I had become a fan of the show in 1991, I was able to view the series as it was meant to be--one episode a week, not knowing what would come next. As I'll discuss later, this was--ironically--the point at which I began to emerge from the shadow that fandom had cast over my *Doctor Who* experience.

3

FIFTIETH ANNIVERSARY BINGE: AN INTRODUCTION

Rather than torment you with a list of episodes, plot summaries, and recycled backstage anecdotes, accompanied by a few thoughts on every story I am attempting something a bit different. What follows in this section is a brief essay on some aspect of each era of the show. While I watched every extant episode as background to these essays, I will not be commenting on every story. Instead, where a certain story informed my thinking on a particular topic, I'll discuss that. To be thoroughly honest, not every episode or story stuck in my head (for example, there is little about "The Keys of Marinus" that has remained with me over the months between watching it and writing this book). I am hoping that this makes the book a bit more readable and--to be frank--this approach has made it much more writable.

There are some other caveats: I barely could find time to watch actual video, so attempting to cope with finding and viewing/listening to fan-made reconstructions of wiped episodes was out of the question. That said, I did watch every episode that still exists--whether or not the entire story is complete. I watched the original as-broadcast versions (at least, I did when I could. Some episodes have changes to the original version). This means I watched four episodes of "The Curse of Fenric" or "Enlightenment" rather than the "feature-length" edits available on the DVDs. "Silver Nemesis" was unavailable to me without the extended scenes. If it makes you feel any better, it was still terrible. Similarly, I chose not to watch versions with "updated" special effects. What's the point, really? Hopefully, these exceptions are acceptable to readers. They were, mostly, designed to make this job a bit more manageable.

Also, I should mention, there may be spoilers contained in the following chapters. The show's been around for fifty years--I think the statute of limitations is past.

4
THE 1960S

The First Doctor- What Show is This?

So there it is--a weird, stagey, shot-mostly-as-live black and white tale of our heroes (two school teachers) who investigate their student and discover her angry science wizard of a grandfather who inhabits a space-age magic cabinet. The student has a strange, pixie-like, etherial quality and the wizard grandfather is, honestly, fairly unlikable. After around twenty-five minutes, the episode dissolves in some blinding light and strange noises and we're left with the police box magic cabinet standing on an unconvincing landscape with an shadowy figure looming.

"An Unearthly Child"--season one, episode one of *Doctor Who* is an odd episode. It puts in place many of the familiar features of the show I had (by the time I'd seen it for the first time) already come to know and love but it does so in a way that was at a strange angle to what I thought I knew. What is the most clear (as many commentators have stated) is that Ian and Barbara are clearly meant to be the focus here. They are the two the audience is meant to be cheering for, to be frightened for, and with whom they should most closely identify. This is, probably, the most striking difference between this opening episode and the show *Doctor Who* would eventually become.

The show begins to take on something more closely resembling its eventual shape a few episodes later with the arrival of the Daleks. But it isn't until Susan's departure and the arrival of Vicki that many of the tropes we (for better or worse) take for granted begin to fall into place. With "The Chase" and the exit of Ian and Barbara the show is finally fully the Doctor's. The show had been moving in that direction for a while (particularly after "The Edge of Destruction"/"Inside the Spaceship") But up through "The Chase" *Doctor Who* is an ensemble show. Beginning with ""The Time Meddler", at the end of its second "season"[4] *Doctor Who*

---

4. Even the concept of "seasons" is nebulous and not what we would expect at this point. As the show ran (and ran, and ran, and ran) for the majority of the calendar year, what we refer to as seasons might not have seemed so to the audience. In many cases, the

becomes the story of the Doctor and his revolving door cast of companions. The Doctor, like all well-drawn characters, always assumed he was the hero of his own story, even when he was risking his companions' lives on Skaro or contemplating bashing in caveman skulls. With the departure of Ian and Barbara, however, the writers and producers of the show must fully embrace the Doctor--an increasingly lovable grump--as the hero.

So at its beginning, *Doctor Who* was not necessarily the show we "remember." It was not even the show we "remember" a month later when Nation's and Cusick's plunger-wielding tin cans make their first appearance. We remember *Doctor Who* mostly in the sense that we view it through the lens of our fandom. We come to a conclusion about what best exemplifies "good" *Doctor Who.* In some cases, the more dogmatic of us break things down in to "real" Doctor Who and "not really" *Doctor Who.* This is usually a function of our initial exposure to the show. For Americans--at least during my initial period of exposure to the show--this meant the Tom Baker era. For me, it was the McCoy years and the range of Virgin's New Adventures.

So what does this have to do with William Hartnell, the early 1960s, and the creation of the show? One thing I

---

production schedule of the show did not necessarily follow the season breaks we've come to acknowledge.

noticed as I watched these earliest serials is now easy (and lazy) it would be to pigeonhole the various stories into the taxonomy that fandom developed in the 1980s. We may view "Marco Polo" is a historical; "The Edge of Destruction" is an oddball story (like "The Mind Robber" or "Warriors' Gate"); "“The Time Meddler" is a pseudohistorical (like "The Time Warrior" or "The Visitation"); "The War Machines" is a modern-day Earth-based story where the Doctor cooperates with political and military authorities ("clearly a pre-cursor to the Pertwee years"). This atemporal way of viewing the development of the show has, I think, done the Hartnell years a disservice. "Good" stories are ones that fit what we think the show should be doing. "Bad" stories are ones that don't conform to our vision of Doctor Who. There is, of course, an additional problem. For so long, fans had little first-hand exposure to the stories, knowing about them only from summaries in program guides and *Doctor Who Magazine.* We absorbed the opinions of those who reviewed the stories, without having the means to form our own opinions. For those who, like I did, received their knowledge of the show's past from sources like Peter Haining's coffee table books and *DWM* reader surveys, it was quite a shock to realize that "The Gunfighters" was actually really good.

So imagine my surprise when I found that the Hartnell era has become--by a wide margin--my favorite. Even

"The Space Museum." No. Especially "The Space Museum"--I love it. I know the standard view has been one of the first episode being mind-bending "sideways-in-time" stuff, let down by the subsequent three episodes of running around, getting captured, escaping, and dealing with incompetent bad guys and useless good guys.

Rather, I think "The Space Museum" is a fun, lightweight piece that explore the nature of time and--and this might be a stretch--the bizarre, confusing, and dangerous life the Doctor, Ian, Barbara, and Vicki live. "The Space Museum," (despite the banality of the Moroks and the relatively quick and easy escape from danger) illustrates that life in the TARDIS puts its crew in situations where they might be killed, frozen it time, or otherwise eliminated in ways we cannot even begin to imagine or understand. On a week-to-week basis, forty-odd weeks a year, anything can be a threat. The Doctor can be baffled (and wrong). Vicki can be an inspiring revolutionary leader. "The Space Museum" is one of the best examples of how--at its best--the show in the Hartnell years was a weekly excursion into something that was like nothing else on television and, often, not even very like itself.

As production teams changed, so would the focus. But, on the whole, Lambert, Wiles, and Lloyd (aided by script editors Whitaker, Spooner, and Tosh) had the fewest preconceived notions about what Doctor Who could (or could not) do as a piece of low-budget serial family entertainment. In the subsequent years, the show would become more formulaic, more predictable and more like the notional *Doctor Who*[5] with which we're all familiar (whatever that might be).

It's not just because I'm naturally drawn toward historical-type subjects that I think the Hartnell era might be my absolute favorite, go-to eras of *Doctor Who.* William Hartnell is amazing. He's just wonderful as the original Doctor and every actor since has been in his shadow. Despite the fluffs[6], despite his oft-reported irascibility toward those with whom he worked, he was amazing. His co-stars were equally great. There has never, in my opinion, been a better audience identification figure than Barbara. Vicki did the whole

---

5. The term "notional *Doctor Who*" is one that I picked up from reading Lance Parkins's work (best collected in the first volume of Mad Norwegian's Time Unincorporated series) and I think its a useful way to think about the individual conceptions of what "real" or "good" *Doctor Who* we carry with us in our heads.
6. Although, listen to the audio of "The Massacre of St. Bartholomew's Eve" and you may wonder how many of those fluffs were truly mistakes and how many were affectations. When he had to, Hartnell could blow it out of the water.

"future-girl" companion in a way that just makes me smile. Throughout the Hartnell years (and the Troughton ones, to be fair) there is a sense that the actors are playing it completely seriously. Sadly, one cannot consistently say that of the show in the 1970s and 1980s.

There were missteps, yes. I still cannot really watch all six episodes of "The Web Planet" without wandering off to do something else. "The Celestial Toymaker" is tedious and cheap-looking, despite its reputation in some circles. I cannot stand Dodo and, if I'm honest, I always found Susan's character to be used and written poorly. Her performance (and the lines she was given to say) never reached the standards set out in that first episode. And of course, like the Troughton era (although not to the same extent), BBC video destruction policies mean that we cannot get the complete picture of the show in the 1960s.

But when I'm in the mood to watch some *Doctor Who*, when the rest of the family lets me, I tend to put in a Hartnell story. I could watch "The Romans" everyday. I think "The Rescue" is the best companion introduction story ever and is--even if he did not realize it--a template for Russell T. Davies's "Rose." I would rate Hartnell's comedic sense right up there with Tom Baker's (again, "The Romans").

Above all, it makes me happy; happier than any other era of the show. Try as I might, I cannot quantify it or explain it in any reasonable way. Rather than trying, I think I'm going to go watch "The Space Museum" for the thousandth time.

The Second Doctor- New Boy

I often wonder, apart from what we can read in contemporary news accounts and the like, what *Doctor Who* viewers thought at the end of "The Tenth Planet" and at the beginning of "Power of the Daleks" back in 1966. If we are to take as true what we see in the surviving off-screen photos of lost episodes, audio recordings, and memories of viewers, Patrick Troughton's clowning in "Power of the Daleks" must have been a strikingly odd experience for those watching at home, who had become comfortable with William Hartnell's portrayal of the Doctor for three years.

Although.... Even that way of thinking ("William Hartnell's portrayal of the Doctor") is a little ahistorical. Before Patrick Troughton, there really was no notion that there could be more than one portrayal of the Doctor. Apart, that is, from within the imagination of producer John Wiles, who--some say--was the pioneer of the idea of replacing the Doctor, as a way of ridding himself of his troublesome leading man. It is almost cliché to praise the innovative and revolutionary nature of the concept of "regeneration" (not called such, of course, until the end of the Jon Pertwee years) but it *is* a seriously cool idea.

As a fan who did not start watching the show in Britain in the 1960s (since I was, sadly, born in America in the 1970s) there was not much Troughton left for me to watch this past years as I indulged in my epic *Doctor Who* binge. As I said earlier, I only viewed actual video, not audio/still reconstructions, so I watched lots of individual episodes from incomplete stories and...some really lousy stories from season six. Despite this, I feel like I got a decent impression of the various aspects of the Troughton era.

I have always had a strange reaction to the Troughton stories, mostly because my initial exposure to the second Doctor was through "The Three Doctors," "The Five Doctors," and "The Two Doctors." It may not surprise you to know that I thought, based on these stories, that I had a handle on Troughton's Doctor. When I saw my first *actual* second Doctor story ("The Seeds of Death" as, for a long time, that was the only one I was able to get on video) I was surprised that the Doctor was not as goofy, not as catch-phrase-oriented, and not as cuddly as I had been led to believe.

Watching the original Troughton stories, rather than the anniversary stories, I found his character entertaining and--significantly--much more subdued than I imagined it would be. The moments of manic activity were amazingly frenetic and very entertaining.

I think, watching these stories over again, that some of the perceived classics were stories that I was honestly a bit bored with. When "Tomb of the Cybermen" was finally found and released to the public in the early 1990s, I had believed it would be horrific and terrifying. While it is fun and a bit exciting, it's hardly the be all and end all of 1960s *Doctor Who*. On the other hand, the two episodes of "The Faceless Ones" that I was able to see were actually quite intriguing and I really enjoyed the contemporary Earth setting. The scene where the Doctor and Jaimie are unable to enter the airport due to their lack of passports suited this incarnation's anarchic nature quite well. And, even as far as Cybermen stories are concerned, I still prefer "The Invasion," even with the missing episodes.

Most of all, I found the succession of "base under siege"/monster of the week stories to be a bit tedious rather than the unassailable masterpieces I had been led to believe when I was younger. Perhaps, watching 25 minutes a week, stories like "The Abominable Snowmen," "The Web of Fear," or "The Ice Warriors" would have been intriguing. To be honest, I'd rather have all of "The Underwater Menace," "The Highlanders," or "The Macra Terror" back. The Cybermen, of course, came into their own during the Troughton years and I found I preferred them to the Daleks in some ways. In particular,

The real revelation of watching the Patrick Troughton stories over again is the epic ten episode final story, "The War Games." It was tempting to view this as a three hour prelude to the obvious advent of the Time Lords and the Doctor's trial and sentencing. I was pleasantly surprised, as I watched with the closed thing to fresh eyes as I could get, to find that there is a actually a very good, well-designed, fine-looking story taking place before the Time Lords show up. The innovation here was not the Time Lords--they were the solution to the real innovation: a Doctor who couldn't quite solve the problem and put things right.

The first Doctor had, of course, demonstrated vulnerability. It was a vulnerability borne of the character's perceived age and frailty. The second Doctor was, often, portrayed not only as one step ahead but considerably younger and more physically capable. To see him so stretched beyond his limits as to put his freedom at risk was a novel and risky move.

Of course, now we know the production side of thigns and realize that without a drastic change of format *Doctor Who* might not have survived beyond its sixth season. The changes that would be rung for Patrick Troughton's successor would create a new type of *Doctor Who*--with a lead character who was less a mercurial, cosmic agent of chaos and justice than one who longed to be so but was bound to various obligations instead. It's difficult to imagine the second Doctor being beholden to any obligations beyond a sense of justice and a desire to not be bored.

5
THE 1970S

The Third Doctor- What show is this? (Revisited)

As I mentioned earlier, when I first began watching *Doctor Who* in 1991, my local PBS station followed the Sylvester McCoy run with the Jon Pertwee stories, greatly confusing me. Even apart from the notion of regeneration and the fact that this show was obviously older than I had expected, it was an odd experience. Even in the three stories I had seen, it was clear that the Doctor and his companion could go anywhere in time (and space? The novelizations I had found seemed to indicate so, but "Ghostlight," "The Curse of Fenric," and "Survival" had all been largely Earth-based). The military leadership, at least in the form of Brigadier Lethbridge-Stewart was portrayed as trustworthy, if occasionally at odds with the Doctor. This was a shift from the view presented of Commander Millington in "The Curse of Fenric." It was *Doctor Who*, but somehow not.

The Earthbound setting, large recurring cast, and--apart from "Spearhead from Space"--epically long stories made *Doctor Who*'s seventh season particularly different from the six seasons which had come before and, to a degree, the remainder of Pertwee's time on the show. Liz Shaw was a different sort of assistant; not an equal, but not as subordinate as previous companions. There was an endless series of shady government officials, secret projects and strange, almost primeval forces at work. It was very fun, but--initially--it didn't feel too much like the *Doctor Who* I'd been watching. Upon my re-watch of the show in order, was not jarring as they seemed to me previously. For a long time, I felt that despite "The War Machines" and "The Invasion" serving--in fan lore, at least--as tryouts for an Earth-based format for the show, "Spearhead from Space," "Doctor Who and the Silurians," "Ambassadors of DEATH," and "Inferno" seemed far different than what had come before. Upon re-watching the Pertwee years, however, it seems to me that many Pertwee stories, even beyond season seven are much more in the vein of the Troughton "Base Under Siege" type serials than I had recognized.

The main difference is the consistency of the setup for these stories. The "base" being besieged is Earth (or Britain) and, while the friendly military/scientific force with whom the Doctor allies himself is the same from week to week, the villains aren't. It isn't until season eight, with the arrival of the Master, that the Pertwee era really gets into full swing and the format loosens up a bit in some ways and becomes more constricting in others. And while there are some trips off-world, they serve as missions rather than the usual *Doctor Who* formula of the TARDIS crew happening upon something sinister (or, as was often the case, being dragged off course by mysterious forces).

As I watched through all the Pertwee stories, one thing that struck me is the degree to which this Doctor is not truly his own man. The third Doctor's sense of obligation goes beyond his attachment to UNIT. He is also (in stories like "Colony in Space," "The Curse of Peladon," "The Mutants," etc.) an agent of the Time Lords. And while he may have been a cosmic yo-yo, tethered to Earth and allowed out only on brief excursions, his resentment toward the Time Lords is based on his inability to be a free agent. It is not--as far as I could tell--ever really based around an opposition to what the Time Lords want him to do. I think that would have been an interesting angle for the show to follow, actually. What if the Time Lords sent the Doctor on a mission that was just *wrong*? For all the overarching narrative that paints the Doctor as a renegade in terms of the Time Lords, he never (in this incarnation) seems to disagree with their goals or methods--just his place in their plans.

Even after his exile is lifted, he has a new dematerialization circuit and greater freedom, his obligations to Earth and the Time Lords remain in place. In "Carnival of Monsters," for example, he explicitly links the dangers and abuses of the miniscope to work he did among the Time Lords to get them banned. In "The Time Warrior," he invokes the name of his planet for the first time and describes the Time Lords as "galactic ticket inspectors"--a role of which he approves and, given his actions and words in this story, seems to take on as his own. With some clever retconning, one could connect these examples to "Genesis of the Daleks," "The Brain of Morbius," and other later stories and construct a narrative where the Doctor is *never* really free of the Time Lords' control. This could, for example, make the inclusion of the increasing number of stories which mention the Time Lords, feature non-Doctor Time Lords, or take place on Gallifrey part of that overarching narrative of the

Doctor being--subsequent to his trial in "The War Games"--an agent of Gallifrey. This agency, perhaps, lasted far longer than we believed, ending only with the political meltdown of Gallifrey mentioned at the close of "The Trial of a Time Lord." The "Season 6B" notion launched by the second Doctor working for the Time Lords in "The Two Doctors," of course, complicates everything even more.

But this takes us away from what is actually seen on screen in the Pertwee era. Upon reviewing the whole five seasons, I was struck by how much I enjoyed it. Stories that had literally put me to sleep as a teenager (I'm looking at you, "Colony in Space") were much more fun this time around. Part of it was my wider context in media and history. "Colony in Space" was a rancher-vs-mining company western that happened to be on another planet. "The Mutants" was an apartheid parable. "The Monster of Peladon" was smack in the middle of the economic and political crises of mid-1970s Britain (it was still terrible, though). I can't say the third Doctor is my favorite, but I'm grudgingly able to admit that it was not nearly as bad as I remembered it being.

As with so many things, my opinions of the era between the first time I saw it (when I was a *Doctor Who* neophyte) and the most recent time were shaped by the fandom of the 1990s. In the 1990s, as fandom re-evaluated various eras of the show (in lieu of having any new *Doctor Who* to watch), the Pertwee Doctor was dismissed by some as a fundamentally conservative or establishment figure. His love of luxury, expressions of chumminess with the wealthy and powerful and--most of all--his position attached to UNIT rendered him, to some, un-Doctorish. I don't think that these obligations make him un-Doctorish, but they do make him a bit different than the others. One of the key pieces of anti-Pertwee criticism of the 1990s was a 1993 review of "Terror of the Autons" written by Paul Cornell and publishes in *DWB* 112. Cornell refers to the the "clubbish" aspect of the stories with, "Pertwee displaying a worrying knowledge of (token zero-plot material civil servant) Brownrose's boss, Tubby Rowlands" and that Pertwee is "one of the bourgeoisie, a man at home with brandy and cigars." Cornell concludes by asserting that "the new format should have allowed a little more life and humanity into the series. But no, they exiled the Doctor to Earth to become a Tory.[7] *Licence Denied: Rumblings from the Doctor Who Underground* is a collection of fanzine writing edited by Paul Cornell and released by Virgin Books in 1997, contains an article by Amanda Murray which examines the anti-Pertwee phenomenon of the 1990s and

7. Paul Cornell, "Terror of the Autons." *DWB* No. 112, April 1993 Pp 18-19.

concludes that there were actually just a handful of truly significant anti-Pertwee articles and that most of the conversations were debates about these articles rather than the topic itself. After Pertwee's death in 1996, however, things shifted a bit, again. As Murray says

> *Perhaps fandom has changed. It's now all right to actually like the Pertwee era of Doctor Who. . . . We've accepted that we'll probably never see new Doctor Who on television, and we've reconciled ourselves to the medium of the novel and the fan-produced video as the only way we'll gain any new output to argue about. These are offered to us in a more adult format than we have been used to, one we can exert greater control over, and fandom has adapted as it has learned to accept this , grown up, and as a result our perceptions of the series' past, the third Doctor included, have been influenced by a new maturity.*
>
> *New fandom. New Pertwee.*[8]

The notions Murray expressed here go beyond a discussion of the Pertwee years and speak to *Doctor Who* in the 1990s as a whole. There was a sense of fan-

---

8. Amanda Murray. "Pertwee." In *Licence Denied: Rumblings from the Doctor Who Underground.* London: Virgin Publishing, 1997, 28.

ownership of the show and its mythology that I have rarely seen in other fandoms. Partially, I believe, this is due to the nature of the show as a BBC property--and, by extension--belonging to the people of the UK in a way that corporately- or creator-owned shows like *Star Trek*, *Battlestar Galactica*, or *Buffy* could never be. Even with the advent of the New Adventures, ther ewas still a strong sense of a fan-directed present and future for the show. The past as well, subject to the kind of scrutiny that the Pertwee years were, fell under the umbrella of fan dominance.

Fandom, and the shadow it casts, shifts and changes over time. During my growth as a fan in the 1990s I was , of course, exposed to these arguments about Pertwee and the stories produced during his five seasons. These were usually filtered through the pages of the the more staid *Doctor Who Magazine* or through third-hand recitations of other people's arguments on the usenet group rec.arts.drwho. I admit that I allowed myself to fall into the contrarian aspects of this reevaluation. Nothing past season seven, I thought, was worth watching. The harsh dismissals of the Pertwee era stories, the character of the third Doctor and the acting ability of Jon Pertwee rang truer for me because I was not a fan of those adventures--even from my first viewing. When Pertwee audio adventures such as "Paradise of Death" or "Ghosts of N-Space" appeared,

I ignored them. Whenever Virgin released third Doctor Missing Adventures, I was glad of being able to save my $5.95 that month. It never really occurred to me that the snarky, sarcastic, comments of some fans, which I found amusing and true, should be tested against the actual *material*, most of which I had viewed only once, years before.

My re-watch forced me to look at these stories--and the character of the third Doctor--in a new light. And I liked it. Not as much as William Hartnell or Sylvester McCoy, but for the first time I was able to honestly say to myself that I would rather watch my favorite Pertwee story ("Doctor Who and the Silurians") over my favorite Troughton ("Tomb of the Cybermen"). It was a liberating experience and, apart from "Invasion of the Dinosaurs" or "Monster of Peladon," I can't think of a Pertwee I would actively avoid at all costs.

This shift in my attitude toward season seven through eleven is probably the most drastic I experienced during my epic re-watch exercise. I felt a bit sad that I had short-changed so much of the Pertwee era. It's still far from my favorite, and I'd be lying if I said I was not a bit relieved when Tom Baker's face appeared at the end of "Planet of the Spiders," but I'm perfectly willing to admit that I was unfair to that era of the show. If anything, it can be blames for getting lazy, repetitive and dull. But to claim that those flaws were limited to *Doctor Who* in the early 1970s would be grossly unfair.

The Fourth Doctor- Myth Making

As I re-watched Tom Baker's era of *Doctor Who* I was struck by the overwhelming amount of the show's back story which emerged during these years. Much of the continuity to which the should would refer in the 1980s was established during the era of the fourth Doctor. Thus, in several ways, mythology and myth making were a part of the show during this period.

One of these mythologies was the show's own. "The Deadly Assassin" and "The Invasion of Time" would establish the Time Lords and Gallifrey in the configurations they would have in later stories like "Arc of Infinity" and "The Five Doctors." The White and Black Guardians of the Key to Time arc in season 16 would return in season 20. Davros, introduced as the creator of the Daleks in "Genesis of the Daleks" would feature in every subsequent Dalek tale of the classic era of the series. We even, for the first time, discover that the Cybermen were able to be damaged by gold.

In addition to large points of plot or major characters, small things filtered in as well during these years. We hear much more about the Time Lords in stories *not* set on Gallifrey. "Underworld," for example details the reason why Time Lords decided not to interfere in the affairs of other planets and--if completed--"Shada" was set to be the culmination of many of the strands of Time Lord lore. The notion of myth in general appears as well. Stories edited by Anthony Read often made references to Greek mythology ("The Horns of Nimon" and, again, "Underworld"). Even stories like "The Talons of Weng-Chiang" spin myths, with the Doctor's off-hand references to future history. For the first time, *Doctor Who* seems to inhabit a universe vast enough to contain a series and characters of this scale. And, while there are the overt "continuity references" that would characterize later eras of the show, careful watching was rewarded. "The quest is the quest," a line uttered throughout the first episode of "Underworld" could well have been uttered at the end of the Key to Time season, as the key was assembled only to be scattered again--it's job complete.

Overall, the Tom Baker years have enjoyed a good reputation within fan circles with the more humorous and literary Graham Williams/Douglas Adams season being particularly popular during the 1990s. I absorbed these ideas which, inevitably, shaped by outlook. A good example of the ways in which fandom and its media outlets informed my views on *Doctor Who* is Season 18 (1980-81--yes, this is the 1970s chapter, but

I'm keeping this here!). These seven four-part stories were Tom Baker's last as the Doctor and John Nathan-Turner's first as series Producer. This was a strange sort of transitional year for the show, as Nathan-Turner felt a need to eliminate what he saw as overly-humorous elements of the show, particularly Tom Baker's performance as the Doctor. Nathan-Turner had been on the show's crew as Production Unit Manager for several years; he was not a newcomer to the show or to television. Key to Nathan-Turner's approach was his script editor, the scientifically-minded Christopher H. Bidmead.

In 1992, early in my fandom, I read an article in *Doctor Who Magazine* called "Change and Decay," written by Philip McDonald. The article discussed the concept of entropy which pervaded the season. As I had not seen any episodes of season 18 at the time (my PBS station hadn't reached that point yet and there were no official BBC videos at the time), the article made every single one of the stories sound massively impressive. An umbrella theme about physical and philosophical breakdown? "Sign me up!" I thought. Confusingly, in that same issue was Gary Russell's review of "Logopolis" (which *had* been released on video in the UK--I was bitter about that, honestly). Russell was largely derisive of the story, describing it as "overrated, glossy, waffle." I was left deeply confused--one writer may "Logopolis" sound great but another made it sound horrible. As I read more issues of DWM, I found that this was not an unusual situation. Fans seemed to have their own lists of best, worst, or classic stories and these lists rarely agreed with each other (with notable exceptions being "City of Death," "Genesis of the Daleks," and "Caves of Androzani").

I set out on a quest to experience season 18- this Tom Baker season which didn't fit with the other six. Initially, I had to rely on novelizations but eventually I saw each of the six stories. I found my opinion of them shifting over the years. Sometimes I would find myself in the camp that viewed this season as a great shift in tone for the series. Other times, I sympathized with the point of view that these stories were--overall--pretentious, dull, and crass. On my recent viewing marathon, though, I found my own opinion split. I was unable to have *one* opinion about the *entire* season. My current view is that season 18 is an uneven collection but I love it despite that. "Meglos" is yawn-inducing but the sequence that kicks off with "Full Circle" is a whole lot of fun and Tom Baker's increasing weariness and anger is a delight to watch. The mythic aspect, however, began to decline, with broad space-scapes of hidden histories replaced by fairly concise and bland references to things that had happened in various stories in the past. It gave the impression of being broad and mythic but to me, on re-watching, it seemed smaller, somehow, to hear references to things that I had seen than to hear references to things that suggested a vast universe that the series could *never* show.

6
THE 1980S

The Fifth Doctor: Marooned

I really enjoyed Peter Davison's portrayal of the fifth Doctor. Soft-spoken, wry when he needs to be, desperate to be taken seriously despite his youthful appearance--there was a lot to like.

Pity about the stories, really. With a few notable exceptions like "Kinda," "Snakedance," "Frontios," and "The Caves of Androzani" most of the Davison-era stories flowed into a bland series of set pieces repeated from episode to episode from season 19 to season 22. Bickering in the TARDIS, people in jumpsuits, more (and more graphically portrayed) violence than ever, and a Doctor character who seems to be marooned in a show that is called *Doctor Who* but bears very little resemblance to what has come before. Despite producer John Nathan-Turner's assertions that the humor was there but it was "wit rather than slapstick" and that if fans thought that the old stuff was better it was because "the memory cheats," as I watched the stories in order and saw the shift from "The Horns of Nimon" to "The Leisure Hive" and especially from "Logopolis" to "Castrovalva" that something was missing. Yes, I suppose it was *Doctor Who*, but it was "1980s *Doctor Who*," which was just...different.

Which is, of course, ironic, because the production team often made comments about the show "returning" to what made it popular in the old days before things got overly silly under Graham Williams and Douglas Adams. One of the aspects of classic Doctor Who (particularly during the 1980s seasons) that I have cooled on considerably over the past twenty years--and this really came through to me as I re-watched those stories--was the use of continuity references to placate/pacify/amuse/titillate fans. When I was younger, and I heard the reference to the Terileptils (from "The Visitation") in "The Awakening" I thought it was pretty cool. I remembered that story! I knew who those Terileptils were! I was smart!

But on re-watching "The Awakening," I found myself annoyed that Script Editor Eric Saward felt the need to namedrop something from one of his stories into a different story where it was not needed. That said, I do not get as bent out of shape over continuity references as some fans. I do not believe that an over-reliance on continuity alienating the general public was the key reason behind the show's decline in the 1980s. When continuity references become the entire reason a story exists, though, that's obnoxious. Whether it's long-term continuity ("Let's use references to old Cybermen stories to give the new Cybermen a motivation in 'Earthshock!'") or short-term plot-hole-filling ("We need to introduce Peri, write out Turlough, kill the Master, and get rid of Kamelion! On Lanzarote!") there are good and bad ways to do it. Of course, this being *Doctor Who*, it is difficult to get any two fans to agree on which stories do this better than others. One story from the Davison years that I either love or hate, depending on my mood is "Resurrection of the Daleks."

Although I deliberately set out to not have this book turn into yet another blow-by-blow Doctor Who episode guide, I found myself jotting down thoughts as I watched the story. I found that, in general, it held up well, although there were bits that I found quite troubling, given what was to come in the next year of the show. Plus, this story is a good example of the continuity overload of the mid-80s, as the story is a sequel of sorts to "Destiny of the Daleks" and a prequel of sorts to "Attack of the Cybermen." so come along for a largely stream-of-consciousness journey (cleaned up for easier reading, I hope) along with the Doctor, Tegan, Turlough, and our favorite mutated pepperpots.

> *A scene at the beginning of episode one sums up exactly why my wife just can't watch this show. During the opening filmed scenes she said "this looks like the most realistic Doctor Who I've ever seen." I agreed and talked about the virtues of film versus video and the value of modern-day settings filmed on location. Then a bunch of guys in funny jumpsuits came running out the door and got shot. Game, as they say, over.*
>
> *So much gunplay--and not just ray guns but regular bullet firing guns, which I have no problem with in general but they don't seem to belong in Doctor Who. It is nice to see a multicultural cast however. That's something that you think one would see a lot more of in the mid-1980s Doctor Who but you really don't (not until the McCoy years, anyway). Some other problems with this episode: melted faces are off-putting; I don't like the army being involved when it's not UNIT (plus the uniforms are a little odd. For*

example, the Colonel with the one collar out of the sweater looks sloppy (and not in an intentional, "let's make the Colonel look sloppy" way) and the sergeant who just sort of stands around looks a bit lost. It's like casual day at the army. I must say, however, that watching the DVD version is far better than my recorded PBS version. This version has the sound effects on the ray guns and as always the cliffhangers make the show much more dramatic. Even when it's not.

Tegan got a minor scratch. I'm very concerned.

So many soldiers. Even the non-soldiers act like soldiers.

More melted faces. I really don't like the melted faces and I really think the story could have had people dying from the scary poison gas without the melted faces. This is, however, the Eric Saward style of body horror which would come to typify Doctor Who in the 1980s. "Frontios," with its human head slaved to a big drill effect is another good example. Season 21 is a small teaser of what would come in the next year. In many ways this story is a pilot for season 22.

As an aside, I find myself less and less impressed with the Eric Saward style of stories than I had been in the past. Even when lousy, the regimes of past script editors had consistent themes which set them apart from others. Antony Read's mythologizing, Douglas Adams's use of humor, and Christopher Bidmead's science-based fantasy all seemed to be about something. Saward just adds guns and calls it a day. That might be a bit unfair but watching the stories he scripted makes it easier to pick out what he may have added to the stories of others. Certainly, interviews with him since the 1980s highlight that, out of necessity, he re-wrote many of the scripts that eventually made it on the air. I'm not certain that his contributions were always useful, as they usually involved out-of-place tag scenes in the TARDIS where characters recapped past adventures and bickered a bit. This would reach nearly-intolerable (for me, anyway) levels during the Colin Baker years. In any case, lest this seem like ill-tempered Saward-bashing, the man had an incredibly difficult job. In may ways, I think following the Tom Baker years might have been a greater challenge than re-tooling the show for the 21st century.

The helmets with the Dalek eyestalks are the stupidest looking things ever.

Why is Colonel Archer using a pay-phone? I assume there's a reason but I've missed it.

Why Is Turlough given nothing useful to do? Come to that, why is Tegan given nothing useful to do? I could go further- why is the Doctor given nothing useful to do?

The Doctor should not be carrying a gun. There's not even any pretense that the Doctor is carrying a gun ironically or to make a point--it's just the Doctor carrying a gun. The Doctor doesn't not carry a gun because the doctor is weak. The Doctor doesn't carry a gun because carrying a gun is fundamentally uninteresting from a dramatic point of view. I, of course, acknowledge that the Doctor is not above and never has been above getting other people to use guns on his behalf but having the Doctor himself carrying a gun and using it just doesn't make sense.

Davros is making a crucial point about capital punishment vs. perpetual imprisonment. EDGY. RELEVENT. TASTE THE ANGST!

There's some terrible acting in the story. Not from the regulars, though. Davison, Fielding, and Strickson are awesome as ever. I really could have used another have season of this cast.

Terry Molloy is pretty good as Davros.

"This warehouse is under martial law" is the least threatening sounding line ever.

Well, here's the Doctor with another gun. But no shooting, because the episode ends.

I am so tired of Turlough and the random uniformed humans wondering around for no reason. Oh. They're trying to find a self-destruct. That's interesting.

Davison is awesome.

Did Davros always have all the sparkly lights? It looks ridiculous.

The problem with the 1980s continuity-fest version of Doctor Who is that they keep screwing it up, such as forgetting Leela in the flashback sequence.

The sets are pretty good though. It's not lit as brightly as "Warriors of the Deep," or most of season 22.

Still working on that self-destruct. We're straddling the line between padding and plot development.

An irritating point in the "duplication" scene. "The Doctor without his companions would be rather incongruous." Except for "The Deadly Assassin." Wow--now who's the continuity-obsessed uber-geek?

I do like the notion (introduced by Russell T. Davies in one of the Doctor Who Annuals, back in 2005, I think) of this story being another link in the whole chain which leads to the Time War-- Time Lords fired the first shot in "Genesis," and the assassination of the high council represents the Daleks' counterstrike (with the Movellan War being an interruption which made the Daleks ever more desperate).

Oh, now the Doctor is pointing a gun at Davros for a long time without doing anything. What is Saward's obsession with turning the show into a roided-up action series?

Does everyone die in this story, except Lytton and his policemen? Speaking of Lytton, do he and the Doctor ever actually meet? If not, how does the sixth Doctor know who he is in "Attack of the Cybermen"?

Tegan's leaving, seemingly out of nowhere, is a good scene. I question when traveling with the Doctor was ever "fun" for her, though. If all the deaths were an issue, I would think she'd leave at the end of "Warriors of the Deep" because of, you know, the chemical-weapons induced mass murder. If nothing

> *else, she could have jumped ship in 1984 with her grandfather in "The Awakening." From the production side, though, we're tying up loose ends. Turlough will go in the next story, Peri will arrive, and the sixth Doctor will emerge. Watching from week to week in 1984, it must have seemed like an exciting time of change.*

As with most other Eric Saward stories, "Resurrection of the Daleks" is far better when I don't think about it so much. There is much to admire here--the story makes just barely as much sense as it needs to, the Daleks are intimidating, Davros is pleasantly insane, and the Lytton character is interesting. There was far worse in season 21--"Warriors of the Deep," for example. There was also, of course, the worst episode of the entire series: "The Twin Dilemma".

The Sixth Doctor: I Really, Really Tried

For most of the 1990s, in the early days of my fandom, I asserted loudly and longly that the Colin Baker era of *Doctor Who* was underrated, unappreciated, and deserving of far more respect than most fans had given it. Looking back on that opinion--which my reviewing of the series had erased forever--I can only think of two reasons why I might have felt that way.

The first is that I thought it was cool to be different from everyone else. It was pretty juvenile.

The second--and more defensible—reason is that (like Hartnell, Troughton, Tom Baker, and Davison) my first exposure to Colin Baker's Doctor was through the Target novelizations. Particularly Eric Saward's novelization of "The Twin Dilemma." This book was incredibly fun and I re-read it as I re-watched the episode. The book was full of Douglas Adams-like humor which I found very entertaining when I was in ninth grade. While the plot was just as thin as the televised version, the characters were much more richly drawn and there was a lot more background to fill out the lack of actual story. Azmael, in the novelization, was a renegade Time Lord who had committed mass murder, wiping out a number of corrupt members of the High Council. On the television show he was just a doddering old man who really had no clear reason to be there at all and certainly no reason to be a Time Lord. My high opinion of the sixth Doctor era was largely formed by the very well-written novelizations to which I was exposed. When I finally saw the televised stories I was in a quandary. How could the books that I found so enjoyable have come from television that was so dreadful? The one exception to this was "Vengeance on Varos," which looked good, had (mostly) good dialogue, and seemed to be making a larger point about the media without being horrendously overwrought (like the vegetarian message in "The Two Doctors," for instance).

For the most part, the Colin Baker stories were overly violent, needlessly convoluted, poorly written and looked dreadful on screen ("The Mark of the Rani" being an exception as the location filming was gorgeous). Baker's performance as the doctor was, however, very good considering what he was given to do. The plan of making the doctor fundamentally unlikable with the idea that sometime in the future we come to understand more fully why he was like that would be derailed by the 1985/86 hiatus.

The "Trial of a Time Lord" season should have been a triumphant return of the show with a revamped production team and a revitalized Doctor. What I got, when I popped in the DVD, was another series of banal 1980s *Doctor Who* rendered more annoying by the "Trial" framing device which interrupted the flow of the stories and an ending that--when we got to the end of episode 14--made no sense. Yes, I understand that the departure of Eric Saward and the death of Robert Holmes (as well as the contentious relationship between Saward and John Nathan-Turner) meant that part 14 was hastily re-written by Pip and Jane Baker. It was likely that Saward's version would have made as little sense as what made it onto the screen, given how I've disliked most of his output as writer or editor. During the re-watch of seasons 22 and 23, I had warmed up to the sixth Doctor and was sad to see him go, because it seemed like a wasted opportunity. But it was exciting to welcome in the next era. Would season 24 wash away the bad taste of the Saward years?

The Seventh Doctor: Full Circle

So I was back with the Doctor I had started with. Of course, it would be a while before I got to "Ghostlight," the story that kicked the whole thing off but, still, I was excited. The excitement was abated, however, by the fact that I had to sit through "Time and the Rani."

While I referred to "The Twin Dilemma" as the worst story in *Doctor Who*'s history I think "Time and the Rani" may be tied for first place. "The Twin Dilemma," in my mind, just edges it out due to the tone it set for the following two years of the show. "Time and the Rani," on the other hand, is simply a really *really* bad episode. It did not (despite what some detractors say) have a noticeable influence the remainder of season 24 and is certainly not representative of the subsequent two seasons.

I should probably take a moment to show my cards just to get things out in the open. I am a huge fan of the Sylvester McCoy era of *Doctor Who*. I think it might be my favorite out of the entire classic run (with the exception of the William Hartnell years). I think it's criminal the series was stopped after season 26. I think there is far more for a fan to enjoy in these last three seasons of the show then the previous five seasons put together. While most of the 80s concentrated on retreading various parts of *Doctor Who* mythology, the Sylvester McCoy years systematically dismantled or altered this mythology.

From destroying Skaro to re-imagining UNIT, this era brought new life to the table. Even stories like "Delta and the Bannermen" or "The Happiness Patrol," dismissed by some fans as silly or inconsequential, actually demonstrated that *Doctor Who* (as in the Hartnell era) was a show that was capable of going anywhere and doing anything. I love the relationship between the seventh Doctor and Ace. I love the fact that there is an ongoing character arc for the companion for the first time in a long time. Like so much good *Doctor Who,* stories like "Paradise Towers," "Dragonfire," "Greatest Show in the Galaxy," and "The Happiness Patrol" create (or at least hint at) interesting worlds and then add the Doctor. Once again the Doctor is a mysterious traveler. Yes he's a traveler who seems to be going more on "missions" rather than simply blundering in to places but that's part of the reinvention--part of the continually evolving mythology.

Season 26 was the end of the classic series, but also in many ways a high point (at least of the 1980s). For the first time in a long time we had a Doctor we really couldn't figure out. In stories like "Ghostlight," "The Curse of Fenric," and "Survival" was he manipulating Ace for a larger purpose? Or was he just being some sort of weird alien jerk? It was hard to tell, sometimes and there were multiple interpretations. For the first time in a long time, there was ambiguity in the show.

While the series was curtailed at the end of 1989, the seventh Doctor's adventures continued in Virgin's New Adventures series. I'll talk about these books a bit when I discuss the 1990s but suffice it to say that the seventh Doctor's era would continue to grow and evolve and change. Not only always in ways that I thought were particularly good. But growth is better than death.

7
THE 1990S

The New Adventures

Soon (well, a couple years) after the end of the televised adventures of the Doctor and Ace, Virgin Publishing, which held the publishing rights to *Doctor Who* from the BBC, obtained permission to create original full-length novels which would serve as the continuation of the series. At least, that was the intention. A goodly portion of fandom (to judge by polls in *Doctor Who Magazine*) did not read these novels or accept them as "canon"--as part of the "real" story of *Doctor Who*.

Regardless of their status within the larger picture of *Doctor Who*'s narrative, the New Adventures, published from 1991 to 1997, represented a key part of my life as a fan during those years. While I had not been able to experience the show as it aired, I was reading the New Adventures from the moment they arrived (eventually...things took a while to get to the United States in those days). Once Paul Cornell's *Timewyrm: Revelation* arrived in December 1991, truly pushing the Doctor and Ace into realms that in no real way could be made for television, I was hooked.

Even if I was not particularly into every novel, I liked the direction. The seventh Doctor continued in his darkly manipulative path set out in seasons 25 and 26 but with the arrival of new companion Bernice Summerfield (and, later, future cops Roz and Chris) the tone changed. They novels became lighter in tone without losing the essential seriousness of the books. *Doctor Who* could be fun. It could fannishly plug holes in continuity but tell an amazingly good, touching, important story at the same time (Steve Lyons's *Head Games*, for example, which explained more about Mel than I thought I ever needed to know). The worst of the books were over-written and dull. The best rivaled the television series in terms of how I thought about their place in *Doctor Who.* I would never imagine a *Doctor Who* that didn't include "Spearhead from Space."

Neither could I imagine one that didn't include *The Also People* by Ben Aaronovich or *Human Nature* by Paul Cornell. [9]Paul Cornell, more than any of the other authors defined much of the style of the new Adventures. *Timewyrm: Revelation* made us rethink how we understand what *Doctor Who* could do. *Love and War* wrote out Ace (for a time) and introduced the New Adventures first non-television companion, Bernice Summerfield. It also saw Ace engaged in a relationship complete with sexual activity. It also featured the seventh Doctor at his most manipulative and--to a degree--unfeeling toward his companion. Rec.arts.drwho, the internet Usenet group devoted to *Doctor Who* discussion featured some strong opinions about *Love and War*. Bruce Anderson, on January 3, 1993, wrote

> *I finished Love and War last night, and I must say I hate it. Well, hate may be too strong a word. I will say, however, that I disliked it. These books have been pushing the image of the Doctor as some sinister, manipulative thug...half deranged and completely self-comsumed. According to "Love And War" Ace is*

9. Of course, once the third series of the relaunched series came along, *Human Nature*--in at least one form--was officially *Doctor Who*. It was an odd and exhilarating moment.

> *now gone. Is Bernice now to be his companion? I can't say as I love Ace; she's brash, impudent and loud. On the other hand, she is a capable companion; able to get herself out of most scrapes.*

On a more positive note, Daniel Bishop, writing on the same day asserted

> *I liked Love and War. I liked the way Ace left the TARDIS...temporarily mind you... because Sylvester McCoy's Doctor IS always pulling something over on her. I liked the reference from Susan to Dodo to Ace. I liked the Airplane joke reference. . . .In fact, Love and War read more like a TV story than any of the other novels to date, IMHO.*

In fact, looking over the many comments about the book, most people's opinion of it boiled down to their opinion on the characterization of the Seventh Doctor, not just in the New Adventures but in seasons 25 & 26 of the show as well. For some fans, the notion of the Doctor (regardless of incarnation) being manipulative, not entirely "good" and generally alien in a sinister rather than a goofily eccentric manner was unacceptable. From my perspective, I starting being a fan with the seventh Doctor's most manipulative ventures. For me, the blithe wandering-into-trouble approach of the other six Doctors took some adjusting.

Like some of the New Adventures authors, fan fiction writers, and others I began to catch myself reading darker and more manipulative motives into the prior Doctors' stories. For example, I assumed that the sixth Doctor's description of the TARDIS being disabled without Zeiton 7 was a lie (it certainly had never been a substance mentioned before or since) to contrive a reason to visit Varos and disrupt the existing regime, a la "The Happiness Patrol." Rewatching these stories now, of course, I realize that was just not the case. The fact remains that the New Adventures shaped how I viewed the televised stories.

I didn't buy every novel from month to month, but I read most of them one way or another. As the 1990s progressed, novels featuring past Doctors appeared, the BBC took over the publication of new *Doctor Who* fiction and Big Finish began producing full-cast audio dramas featuring Peter Davison, Colin Baker, Sylvester McCoy, and Paul McGann but I rarely found the money or time to consume everything that appeared on the scene with a Doctor Who logo. The 1990s have been referred to as "the wilderness years" but, in many ways, new *Doctor Who* was all around us. Just not on television.

Wait-- who's Paul McGann?

A Return?

Near the end of 1995, those of us *Doctor Who* fans who were on the Internet learned that there was going to be an attempt to bring the show back to the small screeen, on the American Fox network. Airing in May 1996, *Doctor Who* [10] starred Paul McGann as the eighth Doctor, Eric Roberts as the Master and Daphne Ashbrook as not-companion Grace Holloway. The tension was almost unbearable as we all waiting for the show to premier--scrutinizing publicity photos, debating spoilers, and desperately trying to not get our hopes up. There was talk that if the ratings were good, the movie might lead to a series.

I was in Italy for a one-month class when the Fox movie aired. I remember making a very expensive phone call to my dad reminding him to tape it for me and--for pity's sake--to NOT attempt to pause during the commercials! What if he failed to unpause? I'd be ruined! I waited two weeks to get back to the states and as soon as I was back home, I absorbed the entire thing in one sitting, about three times in a row. I loved it. The plot was full of holes, but that wasn't a new thing

---

10. No, there's no subtitle, no episode title, nothing official to call it but *Doctor Who*. The BBC DVD calls it *Doctor Who: The Movie*, but I don't. I'm remarkably rigid about this sort of thing.

for *Doctor Who.* I greatly enjoyed McGann's performance and I will always be grateful that Sylvester McCoy got to do a regeneration into his successor (something--so far--Paul McGann has been denied). Grace was a good, Liz Shaw-like assistant (minus the kissing and other romantic overtones, which I don't object to in principle, I just thought they were gratuitous and poorly done) and the Master was no more ridiculous than the Master ever is. I didn't even really care about the "half-human" thing. I just wish the plot had been more accessible to those Fox viewers who had never seen (or heard of) *Doctor Who.* That--along with having to go up against a key episode of the sitcom *Roseanne*--as well as the fact that Americans who had heard of *Doctor Who* tended to connect it to the cheap and odd things they may have seen on PBS--was a crucial misstep.

Scholars of media culture have attributed this approach to broadcasters' (including the BBC of the 1990s) increasing reliance on demographic research. *Doctor Who*--1990s thinking went--was "cult" television. Thus, it had to be written, produced, and broadcast in a certain way. The 1960s and 1970s idea of teatime family viewing did not really have an American analogue beyond evening game shows like *Wheel of Fortune* or *Jeopardy! Doctor Who*--in its originally conceived form of being a show for the entire household--did not fit into the small range of American shows designed for family viewing. Nor did it have the ratings in the US to convince FOX to push on with what it saw as a niche, "sci-fi" . The Fox/BBC Worldwide attempt to make it fit made many wrong choices.

Of course, what we got was better than what we could have gotten. Much has been written about the various scripts that never made it to production for the TV movie, most of them involving a complete reboot of the series as a sort of generic quest tale. Some of the elements of these early attempts (particularly the "half-human" reference and the idea of the TARDIS responding to humans) remained, confusingly, in the final script. There were too many cooks in this particular kitchen, and no solid, visionary leadership.

That would come in 2003.

8
THE NEW SERIES

I did, in the spirit of this whole enterprise include the new series in my re-watching of *Doctor Who.* I found, however, that I have far less to say about it than I did about the original twenty-six season run. It's not because I did not enjoy the relaunch but rather that re-watching the show was not too different from watching it in the first place. In the interests of thoroughness, I did have *some* thoughts.

The Ninth Doctor: The 13 hour Total Doctor Who Experience

As I worked my way through the first season of the 2005 relaunch, my favorite thing about it was that Russell T. Davies and his associates designed it as a contained experience. [11] Over the course of the thirteen episodes from "Rose" to "The Parting of the Ways," a new fan would be introduced to the Doctor, the companion, the future, the past, aliens, Daleks and, finally, a regeneration. It was the complete package. It would have worked--apart from the emergence of an identifiable tenth Doctor at the end--as a self-contained simultaneous return and finale of televised *Doctor Who.* If a second series had never appeared, fans would have had something more satisfying and wonderful than the 1996 McGann return ever could have been.

Of course, there were complaints from fans. It was too light in tone, the jokes were too numerous and fell flat. There were no Cybermen. Eliminating the Time Lords was a mistake. It was aimed at the lowest common denominator. There was no regeneration to introduce the ninth Doctor. There was praise as well but,

---

11. Whether or not this was intended is another matter. There is a lot of uncertainty about the reasons Christopher Eccleston left after one season and there is some indication that this might not have been the original plan. Tat Wood's "Did He Fall or Was He Pushed?" essay in Volume 7 of the *About Time* series (Mad Norwegian Press, 2013) covers the extant theories and their relative likelihoods quite well.

increasingly, I found myself drawn to the critiques that ignored typical fannish issues of continuity and canon and focused on those that looked more deeply at the new stories.

Lawrence Miles (well-established an author of popular and complex novels for the New Adventures and BBC Eighth Doctor series), in particular, was an interesting case. I often find myself neither agreeing nor disagreeing with his views but rather simply letting his notions wash over my brain and give me something new to think about. One of the best examples of his deeply and carefully considered diatribes was against he 2005 episode "The Unquiet Dead." When I saw the story, I viewed it as a throwback to traditional *Doctor Who* in its form of "friendly aliens turn out not to be." I like the historical setting and it seemed, to me, to be fairly innocuous. Miles, on the other hand, saw deep--and deeply disturbing--political ramifications to Mark Gatiss's story. A post on his blog drew the ire of much of online fandom and Miles replaced the original review with a revised version. Currently, however, the "Mileswatch" blog has preserved the original. The crux of Miles's concerns lies in his perception that the Gelth are analogous to refugees, immigrants, or asylum-seekers:

*I'm sorry. There's no other way of saying it. This is offensive, poisonous, xenophobic **** [asterisks in original]. I know many of you will be saying "a-hah, but there have always been alien invasion stories in Doctor Who, what's the difference?", so I'll tell you the difference. There was never a time in the history of original Doctor Who, not even in the days when polite middle-England was terrified by the thought of being overrun by funny-coloured people, when the programme pandered to that kind of vermin-thinking by claiming that all foreigners were invaders (see, especially, "The Ambassadors of Death"... Enoch Powell isn't welcome in the Doctor's universe). "The Dalek Invasion of Earth" came from the war-time generation's fear of Nazism, not from a terror of immigration. "Spearhead from Space", like much of '70s Doctor Who, shows the invader to be a ruthless, self-involved force modelled on the inhuman instincts of our own culture rather than on swarthy-looking foreign types. "The Unquiet Dead" is different. "The Unquiet Dead" is a story, made at a point in time when the big electoral issue is whether the British should put up with foreigners at all or treat them like scrounging gypsies, about a bunch of* REFUGEES *- about a bunch of* ASYLUM-SEEKERS *- who ask the Doctor for his help and then turn out to be* EVIL ALIENS WHO JUST WANT TO SWARM YOUR COUNTRY NYHAH HAH

> *HAAAAAH WE WILL RAPE YOUR WOMEN AND DEFILE YOUR CORPSES.*[12]

Once again, my position as an American, living in a country where our immigration debates are a bit different than those in the United Kingdom or other European countries, makes things a bit less clear to me. The points Miles makes here, however, are crystal clear. I first realized that my relationship to *Doctor Who* and to the fandom surrounding it had changed. I did not come to the same conclusions but I surely understood how he came to those conclusions.

But Miles's view of "The Unquiet Dead" extends beyond the problems he perceives with that particular episode to a broader condemnation of what he saw the series becoming. Some selections:

> *This is a programme that teaches children never to trust people who look a bit weird, especially not if they're asking for sanctuary from a war that nearly wiped them out, because they're obviously criminals playing on our*

12. Lawrence Miles. "The Unquiet Dead," April 9, 2005.
http://lawrencemiles.blogspot.com/2005/04/unquiet-dead.html

> *bleeding-heart compassion and will always stab us in the back. . . .*
>
> *After two weeks of being really, really good, Doctor Who has become something sickening, twisted and wrong. I can't express how vile and awful this is, so I'll shut up soon. All I know is that I wish the series had never come back, rather than come back like this. . . .*
>
> *A script like this, in 2005, is as disgusting and as irresponsible as a programme about big-eared money-grubbing aliens with Yiddish accents would have been in the 1930s. No, a better comparison: imagine an American TV show made in the late '60s, which claimed that dark-skinned aliens weren't quite smart enough to run their own society and thus shouldn't be allowed a vote. That's the kind of programme we've been given tonight. . . .*
>
> *I feel sick. And betrayed. And God help me, if I weren't already "committed" to this series then this would be the point at which I'd give up.*[13]

I cannot agree, totally, with Miles's assessments, but they certainly made me think eight years ago when I first saw "The Unquiet Dead." To a surprising degree in the re-launched series, has portrayed non-human

13. Ibid.

races in largely negative terms (not, of course, that the original series *didn't* do that). The first season of *Torchwood*, the *Doctor Who* spinoff, gave the impression that *all* aliens were evil to one degree or another.

The relationship between the ninth Doctor and Rose in the first series of the relaunched *Doctor Who* is far different from what we've seen before. There are overtones of love but not necessarily romance. I find that I liked Rose far better in the Eccleston season than I did in the Tennant years. As Rose becomes more self-assured in her travels she becomes less of the "everyperson" figure for viewers to latch on to, which is a solid way to develop the character. Things would, however, soon change.

The Tenth Doctor: Coming to Terms with the Past

As I re-watched the David Tennant years I found myself constantly wondering what a second Christopher Eccleston series would have been like. Eccleston's greatest strength, I think, as the Doctor was being able to play him as a true outside, cut off from the rest of the universe. Rose broke down those barriers, and the arrival of the Daleks forced him to confront the Time War but he is very much a here-and-now character. That would have had to change for the second year but

I'm not sure Eccleston would have been the best choice for a *Doctor Who* that went the direction it did. David Tennant's relatively angst-free portrayal worked well for an era that saw the show grow more comfortable with its past. The appearance of the Master, Sarah Jane and K9, the Cybermen (although with a new origin), and even the return of first series characters like Cassandra, the Face of Boe, and Pete Tyler needed a fresh face.

As the tenth Doctor years continued, new fans of *Doctor Who* were introduced to the revolving companion door that we old-timers took for granted. Martha, I believe, suffered from the very show itself seeming (to me) to be reinforcing the idea that she was not as good as Rose. Catherine Tate's Donna Noble was my favorite companion of the new series if for no other reason that any hint of romance (requited or not) was absent.

Just as the production was coming to terms with the decades of *Doctor Who* that came before, the character of the Doctor also came to terms with the Time War. Or so we thought. The end of the seventh series and the impending fifitieth anniversary special bring the event up once more. As I watch "The End of Time" I truly felt that the mysterious Time War arc was done. We still knew far less about it than most fans wanted to but the crucial element, to me, seemed resolved. The Doctor had confronted the Time Lords, the Master had some resolution to his character and I believed we would move on.

The tenth Doctor era was the one which seems to have brought in the most new fans, at least from what I've seen here in the United States. As we moved into the Matt Smith era, I was struck by the number of fans online and in "real" life who expressed real concern that they would (or even *could*) keep watching the show without "their" Doctor. I instinctively try to avoid any thoughts or words that might set me up as some sort of "gatekeeper" type of fan but I did find it fascinating that regeneration, one of the show's greatest strength and one of the keys to its longevity could cause so much consternation.

The Eleventh Doctor: Miss a Week and you Miss a Lot

Honestly, I do not feel confident saying too much about the eleventh Doctor era. As I write this, the fiftieth anniversary special is months away as is Matt Smith's impending transformation into Peter Capaldi. I suspect that some of the loose ends and recurring themes that have intrigued and/or irritated me since series five will be brought to close on December 25, 2013.

In brief, however, I would be very happy to see an end to episodes that require me to have paid painstaking attention to nearly every previous episode. The recurring "Bad Wolf," "Torchwood," and "Saxon" themes of the Davies years also placed hints along the way leading up to a finale story, but these were Easter eggs and bonuses. If you *hadn't* caught all the Bad Wolf references throughout series 1, then you got primed for the whole thing in "Boom Town" and had it all (sort of) explained in "Bad Wolf" and "The Parting of the Ways." I have found Steven Moffat's conception and structure of the show to be--overall--more complex and intricate than Davies's but at the same time somewhat less fun. The deus ex machina resolutions of the Eccleston and Tennant years got a bit annoying to me but I (and others) were able to be swept along with the general narrative. Davies was excellent at creating resonant emotional moments that transcended the particulars of the plot. Upon my initial viewing, these things rankled. Now I see them as an essential part of keeping *Doctor Who* from drifting too far into cult television territory.

I have a feeling the fiftieth anniversary story and the upcoming Christmas regeneration will serve to clear the decks. Perhaps it is time for a relaunch of the relaunch.

9
OUT FROM THE SHADOW

So where does that leave me?

The show still goes on, of course, with a massive fiftieth anniversary special a few months away, as I write this. Additionally, the factual origin of the series will finally get some love via a television special dramatizing the events, with actors portraying William Hartnell, Verity Lambert, and the rest. A twelfth Doctor has been cast, and I think Peter Capaldi will do an amazing job (and, the older I get, the more I appreciate a Doctor played by someone even older). Its popularity continues apace and I am, for the moment at least, still a fan.

Throughout my Doctor Who fandom, I came into various stories with a preconceived notion that I would either like it or dislike it, based on what I had read in "official" publications (like the Peter Haining-style books), semiofficial publications (like Doctor Who Magazine) or fanzines. There were also, of course, books that I've mentioned elsewhere like the "Handbook" series, the Discontinuity Guide, or even the very recent About Time series. As I rewatched the series from its beginnings, I couldn't help but notice things that other commentators had mentioned--a cultural reference, a performance, or a particular line that I was anticipating. The writings of other fans (and what sets Doctor Who reference material apart from some other more corporatized efforts like those of the Star Trek range is that its authors are overwhelmingly fans) had primed me to look for certain things. Because of Doctor Who Magazine, I went into watching season 18 looking for mentions of entropy and decay. I might not have seen them otherwise or, if I had, I might not have given it much thought until "Logopolis" tied it all together.

Early on in that fandom, when the viewing experience failed to live up--or down--to the expectations I had set, I would sometimes wonder if I was being a fan in a wrong way or, if I wasn't a fan at all. I liked "The Space Museum," but "The Talons of Weng-Chiang?" To use a message board neologism: "meh." Was I wrong? Was I not really a Doctor Who fan? Perhaps--and this is a real possibility--I was simply being contrarian and taking an unpopular view because it was unpopular. My epic re-watch of the series brought back some of these feelings. I still didn't care about "Talons" and I still loved the "The Space Museum." I thought the Troughton stories were fairly dull, but the Pertwee tales had more subtext and substance than I had ever noticed. Colin Baker? Good actor, good Doctor, terrible stories. The guidebooks and received wisdom gave me things to look for, but I began to be more comfortable with my own opinions. I was, after almost 25 years, coming out of fandom's shadow.

As the new series began, however, came a surge of merchandising and popularity that was completely new to me. While there had been merchandising with the 1996 television movie, it was nothing like what happened beginning in 2005. The BBC carried on with a series of original novels but--unlike the Virgin New Adventures or the BBC's own Eighth Doctor Adventures--they were unable (and this makes sense) move the story of the Doctor and Rose forward. They were placeholders; much more like the *Star Trek* tie-in novels than ever before, and more than I was comfortable with. I read a few, but they were inconsequential compared to the dozen years of forward-thinking sometimes shocking story-telling I'd been used to.

So while the show itself was incredibly good--and I think the thirteen episodes starring Christopher Eccleston are among the best runs of *Doctor Who* ever--I found myself drifting further back into the role of being a viewer rather than a fan. I made a concerted effort to avoid spoilers. I did not check out message boards or blogs until after I had already seen the episode. I didn't want to have plot and character twists ruined, of course, but I also wanted to finally experience the feeling of seeing the series fresh. By "fresh," I don't simply mean without prior knowledge of what happened but without any sort of expectation of what I might think or feel about it. During that first series it was difficult to maintain this information abstinance, especially after news broke that the Doctor would be regenerating at the end of the series. I held out, however, enjoying each episode as it aired. I checked out other opinions, eventually, but as the new *Doctor Who* progressed, I moved further and further away from caring what other fans thought of the show.

And so, to a degree, I've moved out of fandom's shadow. Not completely, of course. As I write this, Mad Norwegian are coming out with a new volume of *About Time* which covers the first two years of the revived series. Tat Wood's insight and writing appeal to me, so I'll be picking that up and reading all 450 pages in an evening, most likely. I'm much more comfortable that my own views of the show--and its constituent episodes, characters, themes, and cultural contexts--are just as valid as those of other fans. I have also begun to take enjoyment in a deeper view of the show--looking beyond plot and character to the meanings and subtext that may (or may not, honestly) be there. While, at one time, I might have dismissed the depth of analysis in the *About Time* series as academic over-reaching, I now tend to look at it--even when I do not agree with the conclusions that Tat Wood or his (Volumes 1-5) co-author Lawrence Miles reach--as a crucial part of being a fan.

It has taken me far too long to get to this point but now, in the company of other fans, I can state confidently that I *don't* think David Tennant was a particularly perfect Doctor. I can roll my eyes at Steven Moffat's obnoxiously blatant sexualization of the companion role in Amy Pond. I can be negative when there is, in my view, far too much pressure to be positive, lest the phantoms of 1980s "JNT MUST DIE"-style fandom arise and make things nasty again.

At the same time, I feel perfectly fine being positive. I think the Slitheen were great--a fine combination of fun and menace. I like the belching wheelie-bin in "Rose." I think "The Waters of Mars" is the best single thing labeled *Doctor Who* in the last thirty years. At the time of writing, two months out, I have no fears at all about how the "John Hurt Doctor" will fit into the continuity and larger story of *Doctor Who.* I trust that Moffat will produce something incredible and, if he fails to, who cares? It's only a television show. Yes, of course it is a television show that I love far too much and think about far too much. But *Doctor Who*, unlike *Star Trek*, unlike *Red Dwarf*, unlike *Black Adder* or any other television show of which I've been a fan has made me think about the world around me, and its history, and its culture, far more than I've thought about the show itself. I mean this in all sincerity and with no attempt to sound smarter than I am: *Doctor Who* transcends television.

Most of all, I am now, finally, perfectly happy talking about *Doctor Who* to complete strangers. It is a testament to the new incarnation of the series (but particularly to the longevity, timelessness, and greatness of the original) that more and more people know what I'm talking about. I am still not sure I'd walk up to an acquaintance and explain, at length, all my ideas about William Hartnell, John Wiles, and the notion of generational tension in season 3 but...well, maybe I would.

Just as *Doctor Who* transcends television, our fandom of it transcends the mere watching of a television program. We become better citizens and more critical thinkers. We become better communicators as we struggle to explain just why we believe that "Underworld" is not nearly as bad as some people think it is and why "The Caves of Androzani" might not be nearly as good. We may not--i n the bar, online, in the pages of a fanzine, always agree, but *Doctor Who*'s breadth and depth give us so much to talk about and many, many ways to connect with each other.

Fantastic.

10
PAST AND FUTURE IN *DOCTOR WHO*

The following appending is comprised of an edited and revised version of a couple different talks I gave at the 2011 and 2012 Popular Culture Association national conferences. I've found that scholarly interest in Doctor Who *has grown greatly since the 2005 revival of the show and--in a typical effort to be contrarian--have tended to focus my own scholarly work on the classic series rather than the resurrection 2005 continuation. As a fan, perhaps the best thing I could experience was that the blurred line between my professional life and the interest in the show that I have had for nearly two decades. Despite the difficult scholarly work that such writing entails, because it's about* Doctor Who, *I always feel like I'm getting away with something.*

History, and its related but distinct concept, "the past," are constant presences during the original 26 season run of *Doctor Who.* In the series' early years, it carried an educational mandate and the historical stories of the black and white era served this mandate well. Throughout the series, however, historical settings as well as the series' own narrative past served to convey information or knowledge to the *Doctor Who* viewer. This information encompassed storytelling, characterization, and the desire of the show's producers, at various times, to set out the parameters of the *Doctor Who* universe. The past--the show's own past in particular--was also used as a tool for (lacking a better term) fan pandering.

One can divide these uses of history and the past into two very broad categories-- the historical past and the self-referential past. For the next few minutes we'll explore a few examples--by no means meant to be exclusive or exhaustive--of these types of stories which will, I hope, demonstrate that the presence of the past existed throughout the original run of *Doctor Who* from 1963 to 1989 and provide a lens through which one can examine the narrative development of the show as well as the changing relationship between the show and its fans.

The historical past in *Doctor Who*, by which I mean the use of historical settings or characters, has been part of the series from the very beginning. One example is the fourth story, "Marco Polo," in 1964. Often, these types of stories (known to most fans as "historicals") use history as a setting: the Doctor and his companions arrive in Asia, meet figures such as Marco Polo and Kublai Khan, have an adventure and leave. During these stories, young viewers at home learn some schoolbook history about the connections between east and west in the medieval era. Similarly, stories such as "The Reign of Terror" (about the French Revolution), "The Crusade," or "TheMassacre of St. Bartholomew's Eve" presented historical narrative blended with adventure to inform as well as entertain.

Beyond narrative, however, producers used the past as a means to convey metanarrative. One example of this was the serial "The Aztecs". "The Aztecs", first broadcast in the early summer of 1964, was not merely a story about the historical past but also a statement by writer John Lucarotti and script editor David Whitaker on their perceptions of time travel within the confines of the *Doctor Who* narrative. In this story, the Doctor's companion Barbara attempts to change the path of Aztec civilization to prevent their conquest by the Spanish. The Doctor informs Barbara that she "cannot rewrite history! Not one line!" This not only set up conflict between two of the leads but also sent a message to the viewing audience at home. The declaration that neither the Doctor nor his companions can interfere with established history does a number of things that support both the educational and narrative missions of early *Doctor Who.*

This declaration created a split between the "historical" stories and the "science fiction" stories. If you, as the viewer, find yourself in Earth's past with historical figures that you may have learned about in school, don't worry, the history you learned, or the history you will learn through *Doctor Who*, is stable and unchanging. On the other hand, if you find yourself on a planet other than Earth, or on Earth in the future, or (in handful of cases in 60s *Doctor Who*) on Earth in the present, all bets are off; anything could happen in such a situation.

Of course, setting up these expectations allowed later production teams to subvert them down the road. One example of this subversion is Dennis Spooner's 1965 serial "The Time Meddler." Most *Doctor Who* fans, when asked to name one significant thing about this story would reply that it was significant in *Doctor Who* history because it was the first appearance of the Meddling Monk, another member of the Doctor's society, the not-yet-called-so Time Lords. I would argue that the more significant feature of this story was the notion that Earth's history could be changed. Indeed, the Meddling Monk's plan (and, thus, the plot of the story) depended on this very fact. Here, as in "The Aztecs", the show's producers used a historical setting and narrative to illustrate how the *Doctor Who* universe operated. In the case of "The Time Meddler," the message was that the nature of time was to some degree mutable--that the history with which the viewer was familiar, in this case the Norman Conquest, could be changed. While--within the context of the *Doctor Who* universe--these lessons could be imparted anywhere in time or space, the connection between the notion of "history" and the Earth's past makes imprinting that lesson on the viewer more effective. King Harald was *real*; William the Conqueror was *real*. These weren't the Xerons or Sensorites--the stakes were much higher.

Although the genre of the "pure" historical story would virtually vanish after 1966--surfacing only for 1982's "Black Orchid"--the show's use of historical concepts and settings continued. The historical setting carries with it both narrative and production-related advantages over straight science fiction stories. *Doctor Who* stories set in Earth's past carried with them certain expectations that can be fulfilled or subverted depending on the desires of the creators. 1965's "The Crusade", set during the Crusades (obviously), for example, uses the setting to convey a history lesson, as well as some swashbuckling sword fights and political intrigue. There's a lot packed into the four 25 minute installments of this David Whitaker penned story--something made possible through the use of a familiar historical setting. Viewers knew who Richard the Lionheart was and they had heard of the Saracens. The writer could limit infodump-style expository and jump right into the action. Thus, the historical story, characters, and setting serve the writer; providing a shorthand for getting the average viewer up to speed on who's who. Another production related advantage of the historical setting (whether the story has science fiction aspects or not) is the degree to which the story could be made to look televisually realistic. The BBC's long track record of well-produced historical fiction meant that the expertise and resources for creating, say, a Victorian mansion were more available than those required to create a realistic starship. Hence, one sometimes sees historical settings used in science fiction stories such as "Ghostlight," "The King's Demons," or "The Masque of Mandragora."

Historical settings had purposes in classic Doctor Who beyond simply providing a temporal space for the action and characters. Producers used the past to initiate and continue conversations with viewers about the nature of the show itself and the uses of the past within the show. The historical past also provided a convenient narrative and visual shorthand to convey information to the viewer and to take full advantage of the often meager material resources allocated to the production of *Doctor Who.*

Doctor Who's own past is a historical source which the show plundered consistently throughout its history. Discounting continuity links that were, of course, necessary in serialized drama (starting off a story with a "Golly, that was a close call with the Daleks!" type of reference, for example) *Doctor Who* first referenced its own past in a self-conscious way in 1964 with "The Dalek Invasion of Earth." The list of recurring elements in *Doctor Who*--the Daleks, Cybermen, the Meddling Monk, the Master, UNIT, the Time Lords---is extensive and these types of elements existed in all phases of the show's initial run. During no time, however, were the show's references to its own past more self-conscious than during the 1980s, especially during the Doctor-ships of Peter Davison and Colin Baker.

Starting with some repeats of 1960s stories and a compilation of clips featuring Tom Baker's companions saying "Doctor" as he died ("Logopolis" which also featured the return of arch-enemy the Master) the show's 1980s obsession with its own past spread to the extent that 19 out of 27 (I'm counting Trial of a Timelord as one story) stories featured a significant element from *Doctor Who*'s past. Indeed some stories, like 1982's Earthshock, featured one past element--the Cybermen--layered over another, in this case a series of clips of past Doctors from their adventures with the Cybermen. The origins of this backward-looking trend lie with the positive fan response to backward-looking elements during the first season of Peter Davison's run in *Doctor Who.* Producer John Nathan-Turner and Script Editor Eric Saward, relying (according to some sources--and the behind the scenes history of *Doctor* Who in the 80s is a paper in itself) on the advice of fan advisor Ian Levine, began to ensure that "continuity" references to previous adventures, aliens, characters, or concepts were as airtight as it was possible for them to be, given *Doctor Who*'s long and varied past.

During Peter Davison's first season, these continuity references were fairly limited, but during the next season--the show's 20th--every story featured some element of the show's past as a key element. While this was exciting for fans, having come out of the 1970s, a decade in which star Tom Baker and producer Graham Williams indicated that the show's continuity was a minor concern in the production office, it had the effect of making the show more difficult for the general public to follow. *Doctor Who* has, since the development of a strong, organized fandom in the 1970s, walked a fine line between satisfying two audiences--fans and the general public. Fans in the 1970s, generally, thought the Graham Williams/Douglas Adams era went too far in playing to the audiences. The 1980s would see the pendulum swing the other way--the past would become a tool to tightly connect fans to the show.

While it's easy to point at an anniversary story like The Five Doctors as an example of continuity overload, one need not look at a "special" story to see this in action. 1985's Attack of the Cybermen is a great example of how continuity references--a devotion to the series' past--could easily get out of hand. The story, for those who haven't seen it involves not just the Cybermen, but also a return to their adopted home planet of Telos (featured in 1967's Tomb of the Cybermen). If this were not enough, another strand of the plot revolves around the Cybermen attempting to avert the destruction of their *original* home planet of Mondas (a reference to their first appearance in 1966's The Tenth Planet). And, then, just in case there are any people still watching, the TARDIS lands in the junkyard at Totter's Lane, where the opening of An Unearthly Child took place back on November 23, 1963.

This is a story that makes little sense if one is not familiar with the source material. Fan/critics Tat Wood and Lawrence Miles addressed this continuity-driven story telling in their *About Time* series of books saying

> *[Doctor Who] was not a program for casual viewers. But that didn't matter, because there was a fandom, guaranteed to watch anything with a police box in it. . .at conventions in the 1980s it became almost a ritual that teasing announcements of returning monsters, characters, or writers were greeted with enthusiastic applause. It seemed by 1985 that the programme was made largely to garner this approval.*[14]

Doctor Who in the 1980s was being made for an increasingly narrow fan audience. The increasingly intrusive continuity references and call-backs communicated to those fans that the show was, in a way, theirs as well as the BBC's. References to the show's past rewarded long time fans with a more fulfilling viewing experience. *Doctor Who*, thus, transitioned from a television show for the people of Britain to a "cult" show, made for a group of initiates into the higher orders of *Who*-lore. The message conveyed to fan-viewers was, "This is for you! Thanks for your support--here, have some Silurians!"

---

14. Tat Wood and Lawrence Miles. *About Time: The Unauthorized Guide to Doctor Who.* Volume 5. New Orleans: Mad Norwegian Press, 2005. 315.

Like the historical stories of the 1960s, the continuity usages of the 1980s conveyed meaning from production to viewers. In this case, the continuity references help create a special bond between producer and fans, bolstered by the burgeoning fan commercial culture--magazines, conventions, home video releases, and the like. Whereas the connection created with the viewer in earlier times was based on a shared heritage of history and knowledge, this new connection was much narrower.

The notion of time travel is so embedded within the fabric of *Doctor Who* that the presence of "the past" often goes, if not unnoticed, then certainly under-appreciated. The past has served a number of purposes for the producers of the show since 1963. Earth historical settings provided an opportunity for producers to communicate narrative information to the viewer about the nature of time travel in *Doctor Who.* Historical settings had the practical advantages of limiting the need for excessive exposition and creating an opportunity for BBC set and costume designers to play to their strengths and create believable settings on the show's limited budget. References within *Doctor Who* stories to the show's own past--"continuity"--both recognized and resulted from a shift in the *Doctor Who* viewing demographic from a general family audience in the 1970s to a more circumscribed group of dedicated fans in the 1980s. Conscious callbacks to continuity created a link between the producer and the viewers, providing those fans with an increasing sense of ownership.

You can't get away from the past in a show where the characters travel in time. Between 1963 and 1989, *Doctor Who*'s producers embraced the concept of the past in a variety of ways which served their own production needs, the needs of casual viewers, and the needs of a dedicated fan-base.

From its very beginning, *Doctor Who* used the concept of the future as a destination, setting, or dramatic tool. As far back as the unaired original, version of "An Unearthly Child," for example, Susan pegs her origins as "the 49th century." During the 1990s, writers like Lance Parkin developed comprehensive--obsessive--chronologies of the future history depicted in the series and its spin-offs. The revamped series visits the future on a predictable schedule. During the 1960s, however, the show presented its vision of the human future in an inconsistent, piecemeal way.

What's so special about the 1960s? After all, the original run of *Doctor Who* ran until 1989 and the revamped version that appeared in 2005 has made the human future a regular stop. I'm focusing on the 1960s because, for a start, I have to focus on something--the history of *Doctor Who* on television is so vast that one has to be ruthlessly specific. Second, during the 1960s, the show's vision of the human future was still very much in flux. Of course, the entire series was in flux during those first few seasons and--during its first three years--one could argue that there was no coherent vision of what a "*Doctor Who* story" was; not necessarily a bad thing.

So in the 1960s, particularly during the William Hartnell era of the show, *Doctor Who* could be a different show every week. The only continuity that really mattered from episode to episode, serial to serial was the characterization of the regulars. Thus, we find the future of humanity presented in several different ways over the course of the 1960s. As early as partway during the first season, the show encounters an explicitly human future. The varied ways in which *Doctor Who* portrayed this during the 1960s illustrate, from a creative standpoint, different uses for the concept of the human future.

Broadly, and with exceptions of course, during the Hartnell era the story of humanity's future in *Doctor Who* existed as a tool to be used, not as a set of criteria to be slavishly adhered to. As a tool, it was used in a variety of ways. For example, humanity's future could be used as a setting; a way to get the regular characters into a storytelling situation without having to provide a great deal of backstory. The future could also serve as a tool for conveying lessons or broader themes. Futuristic science fiction is, in many cases, a lens through which creators comment on the present day. The future could do almost anything the producers needed it to.

What these human futures did not necessarily have to do was demonstrate a connection to any other vision of humanity's future presented by other stories. This means that writers and producers had the enormous freedom to use the future in any way that made sense at the time, without needing to follow the strictures of continuity, creating bespoke environments that fulfilled the needs of the particular story. Fans would, in the future, construct elaborate timelines that attempt to incorporate the totality of future history into a coherent whole but, at the time, a coherent continuity of the future was haphazard and not a priority. At the end of the Hartnell era and during the Troughton era, however, the image of humanity's future would become more consistent but not necessarily more coherent as the show's creators honed in on a formula for what *Doctor Who* was supposed to be and do.

Doctor Who's use of the human future begins in "The Sensorites", during the first season of the show. Here, we can see that *Doctor Who* was still in its "educational" mode, telling the children of Britain about self winding watches. Alongside that, however, it's establishing a future--in this case the 28th century--in which humanity is in the process of establishing interplanetary colonies. "The Sensorites", for the first time, features *non-regular* human characters from the future who play a crucial role in the plot--it is humans from the future who are eventually exposed as the antagonists. Despite its future setting, however, "The Sensorites"--with its psychic aliens--plays off of established British works like John Wyndham's *The Midwich Cuckoos*. *Doctor Who* had already in its short life, taken inspiration from a number of earlier science fiction sources. This is a turning point for the series--as much as the first appearance of the Daleks, if not as flashy--it establishes that humanity has a future.

In a similar way, the human future is a setting in two crucial season two stories, "The Dalek Invasion of Earth" and "The Rescue". In the former, we see the future Earth for the first time. The crumbling infrastructure and iconic vision of the Dalek rising out of the Thames are designed to give viewers the frightening chill that comes from seeing something familiar and comfortable entertainingly wrecked.

Viewers had already seen the Daleks defeated on their home turf--this was different. It's difficult, from our vantage point, to realize just how new this was. The first time a defeated enemy returned, the first time the viewer glimpses an Earth of the future. *Doctor Who*, with this story, and the next, takes viewers into new areas--using those viewers' own expectations of the future as a storytelling technique. While "The Sensorites" showed humanity among the stars, "The Dalek Invasion of Earth" illustrates a nearer, darker future; familiar, yet shockingly different and frightening.

"The Rescue" is another milestone--the first new companion, Vicki, appears here after the departure of Susan. Once again, the future is distinctly British--it is a future designed to appeal to the viewers, to connect with them. Vicki the space orphan is stranded aboard the crashed UK-201 spaceship which features a British flag as part of its identifying decoration. [clip- The Rescue 8:30] Ian and Barbara--and this is worth noting--say the spaceship is from "home"--not "Britain." Thus the vision of the future presented in "The Rescue" is the audience's future. Producers intended Ian and Barbara, from the beginning, to be audience-identification figures. We enter the TARDIS along with them. Together we encounter prehistoric man, meet Marco Polo, and fight the Daleks. By making the UK-201 from Britain, even in the far flung 25th century--by creating an explicitly human, and a British one at that, future--the program's creators used the future as a tool to draw in viewers and make them part of the adventure.

This British vision is not, however, too surprising. As Tat Wood and Lawrence Miles point out in their essay "What Kind of Future Did We Expect?" the William Hartnell era of *Doctor Who* coincided with the age of the *Eagle* comic paper and its star attraction *Dan Dare: Pilot of the Future.* Children of 1963, then, were used to the idea of a British space program, at least in fictional worlds. "The Rescue" as did "The Sensorites" before it, pushed humanity into the stars, confirming the future laid out by *Dan Dare* and similar stories.

As yet, however, the future was a somewhat variable setting. Throughout the Hartnell era, the human futures as presented in these stories, as well as "The Chase", "The Dalek's Masterplan", or "The Ark" all vary. They are futures custom tailored to the needs of the plot, theme, and characters. Whether the story calls for a marooned astronaut, an interplanetary government with a corrupt leader, or a race of enslaved aliens, the show's producers created a future to fit.

This flexibility, of course, ends, or at least takes a break. When Innes Lloyd takes over as producer at the tail end of the Hartnell era, we begin to see a standardization of the future that will persist throughout the Patrick Troughton era of the show. It first appears in "The Tenth Planet"--an isolated base with a multiethnic/multigender crew faces some invading villain. The Doctor clashes with the authority figure, and everything ends up okay in the end. With little variation, this formula will appear in stories like "The Moonbase", "The Ice Warriors", "The Wheel in Space", and others. For the remainder of the 1960s, *Doctor Who* rarely goes into the future outside of this base-under-siege scenario. A crucial exception is "Enemy of the World", which again shows a future Earth in an attempt to do James Bond on *Doctor Who* terms.

Beyond the attempted standardization of the future that comes to *Doctor Who* in the Troughton era, there is a standardization of the type of story that creators believe *Doctor Who* is designed to tell. These are adventure stories with monsters. There is little ambiguity or complexity in these stories--which is not to say they are unentertaining. They are, however, formulaic--and these stories' presentations of the future are a key part of the formula. One indicator of the increasingly formulaic nature is the way that a story like the sixth season's "The Mind Robber" stands out. It exists outside of time and space, in a bizarre dreamscape. This is revolutionary for Troughton *Doctor Who*; but not for the series as a whole--a series which included stories like "The Edge of Destruction", "The Web Planet" and "The Celestial Toymaker".

Within this standardization of the future are embedded concerns of the time. In the late 1960s, one particular example is climate or weather control. "The Moonbase", "Enemy of the World", and "The Ice Warriors" all deal with weather machines, or weather control as a key component of the plot. By the mid-1960s, environmental concerns were on the rise in Britain--it's not surprising the *Doctor Who* stories would deal with issues of climate change just as it had with the dangers of pesticides in "Planet of Giants". What's interesting about the weather control meme in late 60s *Doctor Who* is how often it is used. Like the future settings in general, the concerns expressed within those settings have become standardized.

In the end, so what? Why is the manner in which *Doctor Who* portrayed the future significant? Why is it worth examining? One reason is that it gives insight into the creators' changing visions of what the show was for. During the Hartnell era, there was a sense that *Doctor Who* could do anything; tell any type of story. As the 60s wear on, financial and creative concerns lead to a reassessment of what the show should be doing; what types of story it *should* be telling. Thus, we see changing images of "the human future" as a kind of bellwether for the creative motivations and circumstances behind making *Doctor Who.*

The show's use of human futures also provide the contemporary viewer with insight into the concerns the producers--and, by extension, the public--had about both the present the future. The dangers of a new ice age, over-reliance on technology (eg. T-Mat in "The Seeds of Death") and the like work well in a futuristic story-telling context. Similarly, projecting current concerns onto a future setting is a well-worn science fiction technique that the creators of *Doctor Who* used well.

The future was a moving target for the creators of *Doctor Who* in the 1960s. Without an established, consistent history of the future (and with little desire to create one), producers and writers were free to use the show to explore diverse futures, suited to the stories they wanted to tell.

RECOMMENDED READING

The following are some resources (many mentioned in the notes) I found useful while working on this project. In my opinion, they are essential for a deeper understanding of *Doctor Who* as a whole. Despite the prevalence of books from Mad Norwegian Press, they are not paying me in any way…

Burk, Graeme, and Robert Smith?, eds. *Time Unincorporated 2: Writings on the Classic Series.* New Orleans: Mad Norwegian Press, 2010.

———., eds. *Time Unincorporated 3: Writings on the New Series.* New Orleans: Mad Norwegian Press, 2011.

Cornell, Paul, ed. Licence Denied: Rumblings from the Doctor Who Underground. London: Virgin Publishing., 1997.

Leitch, Gillian I. *Doctor Who in Time and Space Essays on Themes, Characters, History and Fandom, 1963-2012.* Jefferson, North Carolina: McFarland & Company, Inc., Publishers, 2013.

Lance. *Time Unincorporated: Lance Parkin.* Des Moines, IA: Mad Norwegian Press, 2009.

Wood, Tat. *About Time: The Unauthorized Guide to Doctor Who.* Vol. 1. New Orleans: Mad Norwegian Press, 2007.

Wood, Tat, and Dorothy Ail. *About Time: The Unauthorized Guide to Doctor Who.* Vol. 7 New Orleans: Mad Norwegian Press, 2013.

Wood, Tat, and Lawrence Miles. *About Time: The Unauthorized Guide to Doctor Who.* Vol. 5. New Orleans: Mad Norwegian Press, 2004.

———. *About Time: The Unauthorized Guide to Doctor Who.* Vol. 4. New Orleans: Mad Norwegian Press, 2004.

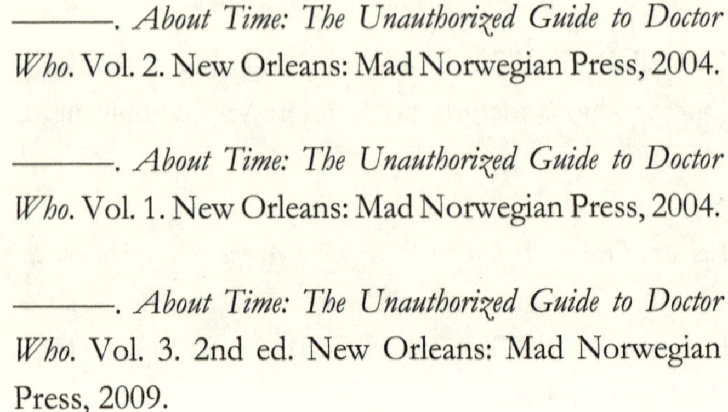

———. *About Time: The Unauthorized Guide to Doctor Who*. Vol. 2. New Orleans: Mad Norwegian Press, 2004.

———. *About Time: The Unauthorized Guide to Doctor Who*. Vol. 1. New Orleans: Mad Norwegian Press, 2004.

———. *About Time: The Unauthorized Guide to Doctor Who*. Vol. 3. 2nd ed. New Orleans: Mad Norwegian Press, 2009.

Additionally, any 1990s fanzines you can get your hands on would be worth your while. The Cornell and Parkin volumes above give you a taste, but the raw, uncut thing is much better.

www.ingramcontent.com/pod-product-compliance
Lightning Source LLC
LaVergne TN
LVHW091009080826
845145LV00003B/1192